Viruses, Bugs and Star Wars

The Hazards of Unsafe Computing

Geoff Simons

NCC Blackwell

MANCHESTER • OXFORD

British Library Cataloguing in Publication Data

Simons, G. L. (Geoffrey Leslie), *1939–*
Viruses, bugs and star wars: The hazards of unsafe
computing
1. Computer systems. Data. Protection
I. Title
005.8
ISBN 0-85012-777-7

Published for NCC Publications by NCC Blackwell.

Editorial Office: The National Computing Centre Limited,
Oxford Road, Manchester M1 7ED, England.

NCC Blackwell, 108 Cowley Road, Oxford OX4 1JF, England.

Typeset in 11pt Century Schoolbook by Bookworm Typesetting,
Manchester; and printed by Hobbs the Printers of South-
ampton.

ISBN 0-85012-777-7

Some other books by Geoff Simons:

Introducing Microprocessors
The Uses of Microprocessors
Robots in Industry
Women in Computing
Introducing Word Processing
Computers in Engineering and Manufacture
Privacy in the Computer Age
Towards Fifth-Generation Computers
Automating Your Office
Introducing Artificial Intelligence
Management Guide to Office Automation
Fraud and Abuse of IT Systems
Expert Systems and Micros
What is Software Engineering?
Introducing Software Engineering
Silicon Shock
Is Man a Robot?
Is God a Programmer?
Are Computers Alive?
The Biology of Computer Life
Eco-Computer: the Impact of Global Intelligence
Silicon Psychosis
Computer Bits and Pieces
Evolution of the Intelligent Machine

Acknowledgements

I have benefited greatly from the work of particular NCC staff (senior consultants, managers, etc). I am particularly grateful to those individuals who have written books for the Centre, and from whom I have learnt something of software reliability and computer security. Thanks are due to:

Joe Abbott (*Software Testing Techniques*)
Richard Watts (*Measuring Software Quality*)
Tony Squires (*Computer Security – the Personnel Aspect*)
Roger Doswell (my co-author on *Fraud and Abuse of IT Systems*)
Mike Wood (various books on computer security)
Ian Douglas and P J Olson (*Audit and Control of Computer Networks*)

Special thanks are due to Dr Ken Wong of BIS Applied Systems Ltd (20 Upper Ground, London, SE1 9PN) for permission to reproduce material from the excellent BIS *Computer Disaster Casebook*. The actual material used is signalled in text.

Again I appreciate the enthusiasm of Wilf Thompson, Divisional Manager, for the present book; and Marcia Lamb, Production Editor, NCC Publications, has provided unfailing support during a difficult and busy period.

Geoff Simons
Managing Editor, NCC Publications

Introduction

A central purpose of this book is to emphasise the importance of safe computing. Today computers are engaged in countless tasks that impinge directly on human life. In such circumstances, computer failures can disrupt social processes, bringing irritation and worse. The more we allow computers to run crucially important activities, the more extreme the hazards represented by system malfunction or system breakdown – and the more attention we should give to reliable and secure computing.

It is important to realise that this book is not intended to be hostile to the use of computers in society. Indeed it implicitly pays tribute to the many ways in which computer applications can enrich human existence. At the same time it is obvious that the benefits of computing will not be realised through inadequate designs, poor software and misguided implementations, and that to use computers irresponsibly can pose many different sorts of hazard to human beings.

The effectiveness of computers can be jeopardised by *unreliable systems* and *weak security*: reliability and security are two of the main areas explored in this book. Attention is also given to the various mischievous and malicious threats to computer systems, dealing with computer crime, hacking, viruses, etc. Copious examples are included to indicate that computer-based facilities face many different types of threat. Thieves, pranksters, political dissidents, game players, etc are some of the sorts of individuals that, when highly computer literate, can threaten computer systems.

It is then important to emphasise that threats to computer systems are no trivial matter, that human life is often at stake. Examples of social hazard are given (attention to aircraft control, hospitals, political aspects, etc), with particular focus on the Strategic Defence Initiative (SDI or 'Star Wars'). SDI is represented as a paradigm of ambitious computer-based systems where failure can result in dire consequences for human beings. Finally a brief commentary on future developments is included. Appendix 1 highlights items encountered by the author while the book was in production.

In summary, we can emphasise that:

— computers are becoming ever more widespread;

— they are being designed to control processes that are crucial to human life;

— software, particularly in complex systems, can never be known to be absolutely correct;

— computer security, particularly in networked systems, can never be known to be fully adequate;

— there will always be individuals and organisations with an interest in penetrating computer security;

— the potential hazards to computer systems, and so to the human beings who rely on them, are sure to increase in the years ahead.

When these straightforward propositions are fully appreciated, it is obvious that the vast bulk of the human race has a massive vested interest in safe (ie reliable and secure) computing. The responsibility lies with politicians, system designers, managers, entrepreneurs, teachers, computer users, etc . . . to us all.

Contents

		Page
Acknowledgements		v
Introduction		vii
1	**The Ubiquitous Computer**	1
	Introduction	1
	The Range of Computerisation	2
	Functional Loops	7
	People and Tools in Loops	9
	Closing the Loops	11
	Factory Automation	15
	Finance and Programmed Trading	19
	Military Systems	21
	Summary	23
2	**System Reliability**	25
	Introduction	25
	Computer Faults	27
	Quality Criteria, Measures	31
	Quality Assurance, Testing	35
	The Future	39
	Summary	41
3	**Computer Security**	43
	Introduction	43
	The Threat Spectrum	45
	Some Disasters	46

Approaching Security 51
Risk Management 54
Physical Security 57
Hardware Aspects 60
Software Aspects 61
Contingency Planning 64
Insurance 65
Fault Tolerance 66
Automated Security 67
Summary 68

4 Malice and Mischief 69

Introduction 69
Computer Crime 70
Hacking 79
Threats from Staff 95
Industrial Action 96
Summary 100

5 Viruses, Worms et al 103

Introduction 103
Background 105
The Life Metaphor 108
Trojan Horses 110
What is a Virus? 111
An Epidemic? 113
The First Virus 114
Specific Viruses 115
Epidemiology 120
Protection from Viruses 122
Summary 127

6 Social Impact 129

Introduction 129
The Computer Impact 130
Vulnerability and Risk 132
Bugs in Software 134
The Political Frame 137
Computer Astrologers 139
Aircraft Safety 139

Health and Hospitals   142
Weather Prediction   143
The Prejudiced Computer   144
Military Systems   145
Problems in Law   146
Summary   147

7   **Star Wars**   149

Introduction   149
Background   150
Profile   154
Launch on Warning   157
Bugs and Reliability   159
Vulnerability   162
Some Objections   163
Summary   164

8   **The Future**   167

References   171

Appendix

1   **Update**   179

Index   193

1 The Ubiquitous Computer

INTRODUCTION

Electronic computers have been around for nearly fifty years, and they represent one of the most dramatic influences on the Twentieth Century. We do not need to tell the much rehearsed tale of computer evolution, the remarkable chronology from massive glass-valve systems of the first generation to the semiconductor-based systems of all later generations. Today, perhaps witnessing the fourth and fifth generations, we see a worldwide proliferation of computer-based facilities: data-processing power is enshrined in silicon integrated circuits (typically, a hundred thousand circuit elements on a simple chip), and no areas of human activity remain unaffected.

This is perhaps the most significant feature of the Computer Age: that the *general-purpose* nature of logic encapsulated in silicon allows computers to operate in any discipline, to address any task, to supplement (or perhaps eventually supplant) any human activity. We are well accustomed to computers in their traditional roles (carrying out banking applications, computing payroll, etc) and to the more recent explosion of small systems in many social sectors (industrial, commercial, domestic, etc). Even so, the sheer ubiquity of modern computer-based systems is not always fully appreciated.

This chapter highlights the modern proliferation of computers in general and the increased tendency to 'close the loops' (using computer-based systems) in particular. It highlights

1

the increasing human dependence on computers, and the corollary (to be developed in later chapters) that such growing dependence makes computer malfunctions – caused inadvertently or by mischief – increasingly important. The growing pressure for 'responsible' computing is in the knowledge that system malfunctions may not only be inconvenient or embarrassing but catastrophic (as with the increasingly massive government and military systems).

THE RANGE OF COMPUTERISATION

Today it is common knowledge that computers are finding applications in every sphere of life in the developed world: the progressive 'computerisation of the planet' is, like computers themselves, a ubiquitous concept in the technical literature and elsewhere. In all social sectors – in office and factory, school and hospital, university and laboratory, etc – computer-based systems are essential, processing appropriate data in dedicated applications, extending the complexity and range of what human beings can achieve. And computers are involved in power stations, sewage plants, transport facilities, communications networks, deep-sea exploration, geological prospecting, chemical analysis/synthesis and weapons technology. They are active in art, literature and music ('computational aesthetics') and in the analysis/development of syntax and semantics ('computational linguistics'). In artificial intelligence (AI), computers are learning how to create, learning how to think, learning how to interpret sensory data, learning how to learn....

It is now more than thirty years since, in 1956, the Logic Theorist program managed to prove 38 of the first 52 theorems in Chapter 2 of *Principia Mathematica* (the seminal work by Bertrand Russell and Alfred North Whitehead). Moreover the program also discovered a proof that the authors had missed. Modern complex systems (eg the Macsyma expert system) are typically more mathematically adept than most human mathematicians. And a growing range of computer systems, embodied in physically small hardware, can exhibit impressive computational power. Today we all know that silicon chips, capable of dedicated performance, can be neatly encapsulated in sewing machines, heart pace-makers, robots, aircraft, calculators, cars, etc. Sometimes there is the suggestion of a growing computer autonomy, an important matter in circumstances where computer failure can threaten human life. For example, the television star Tony Harman considers problems with a computerised car and quotes a mechanic: 'There's nothing wrong with the car whatever, nothing wrong with the computer. Nothing wrong with any of the computers ... they all tell each other what to do' (*The Guardian*, 21 November 1987). And Harman wonders, 'Does the car belong to me, or do I belong to its computers?'

Many computer applications are relatively mundane, though important: involving such tasks as control of traffic lights, management of effluent treatment and the monitoring of environmental pollution. Some aim to model storm conditions, demographic changes or the features of a spreading fire (for example, the Jasmine program aims to predict fire behaviour in new buildings). By 1988, British Telecom had unveiled a computer system able to translate the speech of two people talking to each other in different languages (see, for instance, the report in *Database and Network Journal*, Vol. 17, No. 4, p 3). The aim of such a system is to enable a person speaking one language to converse intelligibly with a person speaking another.

Expert systems, another evolving family of software, have been hyped for several years as likely to impact dramatically on the performance of human experts. It has long been suggested that expert systems will aid human specialists in many fields, and that such computer-based facilities will eventually supplant human endeavour. Thus a diagnostic expert system for engines is described in *Sensor Review* (January 1987). Here it is proposed that expert systems will increasingly *outperform* human professionals, particularly 'in situations that are complex or rapidly changing'. Today expert systems are being developed for political decision-making, chemical analysis, disease diagnosis and war gaming. It was inevitable that much of the early hype should have been misplaced. Extravagant claims were made for expert

systems (and for the exciting fifth-generation plans stimulated by research initiatives in Japan and elsewhere). Today
the predictions are more modest: expert systems are finding
commercial applications, but few computer specialists are
predicting that artificial systems will evolve a generalised
intelligence, over the next decade, to equal that of the average
human being. But again it is worth emphasising the ubiquity
of computers in the modern world.

Computer-based systems are helping to design cars, aircraft, robots and integrated circuits (in this latter they are
formulating specifications for their own functional descen-
dants); to run neo-natal and intensive care units (and to
administer programmes of medical treatment); to control
aircraft in flight (using the controversial 'fly-by-wire' techniques); to inform government policy-making; and to trade, as
money markets fluctuate, in stocks and shares. Again we
encounter a theme – the question of computer autonomy –
that underlies many of the topics raised in the present book.
For many years it has been recognised that a consequence of
computer development would be to reduce the degree of
human control over many types of operation in the world.
Thus Witkowski (1980) argues that it is reasonable for
robotics research to aim at developing a 'totally autonomous
robot under computer control'; and, in the same vein, Chester
(1983) proposes that robotic software should be developed 'to
remove all human supervision'.

Computer-controlled robots, as suitably anthropomorphic
systems, graphically illustrate the progressive transfer of
many types of functional activity from human beings to
artificial systems. There is already considerable successful
research into the design of robots for shearing sheep, playing
the organ, serving as security guards, harvesting fruit,
walking up the sides of ships to paint the hulls (and up the
sides of skyscrapers to wash windows, etc). Patents are
currently being registered, following research at the Agricul-
ture and Food Research Council Institute of Engineering and
Research (Bedford, England), for robots able to milk cows, to
measure the yield, and to detect such conditions as pregnancy
and mastitis.

We are witnessing the rapid development of families of computer-based systems in many operational areas, a circumstance that raises questions about the proper uses of machine intelligence, the nature of man/machine interaction, and the task of ensuring that computer applications are realised in a socially responsible fashion. We should also remember that computers affect different parts of the world in different ways. It is, for example, obvious that computers proliferate in developed countries rather than in the Third World, but there is an equally obvious computer impact on poor countries. The outflow of capital from poor countries to rich, occasioned mainly by debt repayments, is controlled by rich countries that rely upon computers. A multinational petrochemical company with headquarters in the US will know more, by virtue of computers, about the geology of Brazil and Malaysia than do those countries themselves. And the role of computers in the Third World is often far from benign...

Penny Lernoux (1982), for example, in a remarkable catalogue of repressive events in South America, has indicated the importance of computers in helping governments to collect and distribute information on political refugees. In the 1970s and 1980s leading computer companies have sold sophisticated systems to Chile, Uruguay, Argentina and Brazil to aid the apprehension of political suspects for interrogation (and sometimes torture and execution). The National Council of Churches opposed the selling of computers to the Pinochet dictatorship in Chile (the Council director said: 'When you know who Hitler is, you can't pretend you don't know what he's doing with your equipment'). *Computer Weekly* (7 October 1982), in a key article ('How the trade in computers helps to crush human rights'), showed how various international computer companies were directly assisting oppression in South Africa.

Such examples could be extended, but would quickly run beyond the scope of the present book. A principal aim is to indicate how computer failure, occasioned through accident or malice, can pose a threat to human activity *within a legitimate political state*. At the same time it is necessary to emphasise that rich and poor countries alike are affected by the characteristics of computer systems that, increasingly, are networked to straddle the globe. We need hardly point out that, for example, nuclear war – which, if it happens, will probably be initiated by a complex man/machine amalgam in which decision-making computers will play a central role – will bear with equal catastrophe on poor and rich countries alike.

The modern world is increasingly characterised by a *global* marketplace, a *global* financial system, *global* military complexes; and computer-linked communications networks are the effective enabling features of the various globalisation trends. Poor countries, like the rich, are increasingly enmeshed in a shrinking – but ever more complex – world system in which functions, goals and expectations are increasingly mediated by computers. In such circumstances even a single computer malfunction can easily acquire an international significance.

It is obvious that some system malfunctions are more serious than others (see Chapters 6 and 7). A haiku-writing computer that erroneously adds an extra line will threaten no-one's life, but a computer that inadvertently launches a nuclear missile may turn out to be deeply unpopular. In the vast and growing family of computers there will continue to be many applications where malfunctions are tolerable, though annoying and costly. But there will also be an increasing number of automated systems – in aircraft, intensive care units, security facilities, military networks, etc – in which malfunctions will be quite capable of threatening human life on a small or massive scale.

The growing range of computer applications will inevitably enlarge the scope for both *relatively harmless* and *relatively disastrous* malfunctions, but there is no room for complacency about what may be superficially perceived as harmless malfunctions. With the increased networking of systems, a seemingly trivial error at one place may turn out to cause unexpectedly serious consequences at another. There is often confusion about how a software 'fix' in module B will affect the operations of modules P or Q in the same system. And what is true of deliberate (hopefully beneficial) modifications is also true of inadvertent errors (or mischievous alterations) in a system. A change or fault in one place may have totally unexpected, seemingly disproportionate, effects in another.

Before developing some of these points in the rest of this book it is worth highlighting the growing role of computers in modern society. Examples of computer applications have been given. It is useful to consider these in connection with the functional 'loop', the set of procedures that link activities within a domain. With the development of computers, human beings are progressively excluded from the functional loops. This is one reason why, with the increasingly automated loops bearing on matters of ultimate human concern, the reliability and security of computer systems are so important.

First we look at the nature of the functional loops. Then examples are given to emphasise the significance of the loops in human society.

FUNCTIONAL LOOPS

Functional loops ('operational loops', 'activity loops') are analogous to computer programs in that a series of discrete steps are intended, once completed, to achieve an objective (or group of objectives). The concept of the loop, rather than the word, is important: we should remember that computer programs invariably contain their own 'loops' (subsections, modules, etc). For our purposes the important feature of a functional loop is that it represents a means of fulfilling a real-world requirement in commerce, industry, education, defence, etc. It also suggests the idea of repetition, though not invariably. When you follow the path of a loop you tend to arrive at the starting point, whereupon you may choose to traverse the same route again. Some functional loops lack this repeatability: collect data about offensive Western (or Soviet) intentions, conclude that an attack is imminent (or in progress), decide on countermeasures, and launch a stack of nuclear missiles – and you are unlikely to be able to repeat the trick. Other real-world examples, by contrast, represent loops that can survive a first performance.

In the area of factory production (see below), for example, there are many loops and sub-loops that are repeatedly performed to accomplish well-defined commercial ends. At the same time it is clear that the constituent elements of a functional loop can change, disappear, evolve – in the circumstances of changing commercial, legislative and financial factors. Loops may be preserved in a modified form or abandoned, perhaps to be supplanted by fresh loops designed to accomplish newly-conceived objectives. In factory production you take raw materials, process them, shape them, assemble the results, and then add further treatment to yield a product; then you take further raw materials, beginning the loop again.

It should be obvious that the loop can be changed in many ways. Perhaps synthetic materials are substituted for natural ones; perhaps new fabrication methods are preferred; perhaps new design concepts are required to influence the character of the final product. The *class* of product – car, missile, dress, word processor, etc – may remain unchanged, but product evolution is inevitable in a shifting world. And it should also be obvious that the production loop, described in isolation, is a gross simplification of reality. A factory also needs a personnel department, an accounts department, a marketing department, a security function, a despatch department, etc. All these requirements involve characteristic functional loops, with every loop in turn defined by sub-loops.

Nor can we regard the total factory complex as embodying a single overall loop that is independent of the vagaries of the real world. It is inevitable that outside functional loops will impinge on factory activities in many ways. Loops in other functional areas, in other cultures, in other countries, etc merge, mesh, confront and influence, causing reciprocal impacts as evolution occurs in financial patterns, technological developments and human attitudes. It is interesting to reflect that this highly complicated process, operating today on a global scale, is fuelled by the classic cybernetic features – information processing, feedback and a gradually evolving homeostasis.

It is easy to see that there are characteristic functional

loops designed to achieve every sort of practical objective. Thus there are loops for training an athlete, passing legislation, launching a satellite, disciplining an employee, boiling an egg, designing a computer and travelling to a destination. Human competence, expertise and skills have been traditionally recognised according to how well the individual could perform in the functional loops (with 'appropriate' knowledge variously meaning *knowing that* and *knowing how*).

PEOPLE AND TOOLS IN LOOPS

Human society, throughout history, has been involved in functional loops; and tools have been involved in much of this activity. With the development of technology, the tools became more complex, and this in turn had particular consequences. For example, functional loops could be established to accomplish increasingly ambitious ends (human hearts could be transplanted and men could be landed on the moon). Also – and this is of particular significance for the theme of the present book – *the roles of the tools became increasingly important*. Many of the tools evolved into machines, and in some cases – via clockwork, computer power, etc – were able to achieve a degree of independent operation. In this way the concept of *machine autonomy* was born. Computer power, in particular, meant that artefacts were now capable of decision making, information handling, task control, etc. Increasingly the discrete steps in the functional loops could be performed by computer-based systems.

Today, as always, the respective roles of people and machines in the functional loops vary in part according to the level of technology. In the Third World (ie in poor countries) the functional loops tend to be *human*-driven, whereas at the other extreme (ie in rich countries) it is easy to find examples of functional loops that are *machine*-driven. The modern factory environment, for instance, is often characterised by autonomous computer control designed to achieve effective regulation of temperature, lighting, security, etc. Here functional loops can be performed without human involvement.

In most functional loops in the developed countries there is a sense in which people and machines have an equivalent (functional) status. Take human beings out of the loops and the loops will collapse; take machines out of the loops and the loops will prove equally useless. It is clear that, in order to work effectively, modern banking, modern weapons control, modern government decision-making, etc need both people and artefacts. There is currently a functional man/machine symbiosis in which important evolutionary features can be detected. For example, it is likely that, in many of the loops, human beings will become progressively marginalised (see below).

There are now many signs, in the technical literature and elsewhere, of how human beings and machines are being viewed as systems elements with equivalent status. Mantelman (1987), for example, heads an article 'Orchestrating people and computers in their networks' and points out the opportunity that 'awaits those who can mould these technical and human processes'. It is suggested that since people can be regarded as 'nodes' in networks, to study networking technology is to study sociology; and a corollary is that the development of communications should not neglect what may be called the 'people layer'. In the emerging world of data communications we will encounter an 'organically evolving network of people and computers'.

Another development encouraging the progressive evolution of the man/machine symbiosis is that of the 'intelligent interface', the means whereby computer-based systems are made optimally accessible to human beings. We can argue that it is via the intelligent interface that the human being is converted into an effective systems element. Where such interfaces are given an adaptive capability they can accommodate, to some extent, to variations in human cognitive activity – and this activity is itself increasingly interpreted according to the categories supplied by computer science. In short the human elements in the man/machine symbiosis are increasingly seen as systems components: the tendency to supplant such components with artificial elements leads ineluctably to the progressive marginalisation of human beings in the functional loops.

Software ergonomics, associated with the idea of the intelligent interface, exploits insights into human *information processing* and human *operativity*. Again it is essential to evaluate aspects of human cognitive competence: it is no use, for example, designing an interactive system that supplies data (to an operator) that lies outside the limits of human perceptual ability. This work often involves the modelling of human mental processes for various purposes: for example, to show how human mental activity can be effectively duplicated in artificial systems.

There has been much research, as in the Alvey and Esprit programmes, into the nature of communication between human beings and artificial systems. For example, the Media Laboratory at the Massachusetts Institute of Technology is now (1989) in its fourth year of a programme to explore the nature of man/machine interaction. Elsewhere (at, for instance, the School of Industrial Engineering at Purdue University in Indiana) efforts are being made to explore how human beings can function effectively in systems that include industrial robots. There is particular attention to human decision-making as a key factor in determining the scope of artificial systems in which human beings function as crucial system elements.

It is inevitable, in this emerging scenario, that systems needs should increasingly be defined by artefacts: despite the claims of software ergonomics, it is people who will increasingly need to adapt in the man/machine symbiosis. A network in which human beings are a part is still essentially an artificial information-processing configuration. People are regarded as key network components, but only insofar as their capabilities cannot be duplicated by artificial systems. With developments in technology, we may expect the progressive exclusion of human beings from the operational networks, a progressive closing of the functional loops.

CLOSING THE LOOPS

The earliest tools were intended to assist human beings in various ways, as were the more complex machines in later societies. It was perceived that carefully designed artefacts could often outperform human operators, either by performing tasks totally beyond the scope of people or by performing traditional human tasks more effectively. And it was also perceived that machines might supplant some workers while assisting others. This is a central question that underlies discussion of the closing of the functional loops. Put another way, will machines make people redundant? And, for the purposes of the present book, how do we then evaluate our position in a machine-driven culture?

There has long been debate about the likely impact of machines on human employment in particular and human society in general. Early mechanisation had a massive impact on the industrial working developments of the Industrial Revolution in Europe and elsewhere. Friedrich Engels, in his seminal *The Condition of the Working-Class in England in 1844*, showed that the machine impact was often far from benign. The discernible disquiet caused by machines persists in modern times, and all the traditional concerns are evident. Do machines dehumanise people in society? Do they threaten our safety and security? Do they, in the Computer Age, constrain human autonomy and marginalise our decision making? In particular, are computer-based systems leading to a closing of the functional loops in such a way that we are becoming dangerously reliant on automated facilities?

The development of computer-based systems in the 1960s and 1970s caused massive changes in traditional working patterns. In the 1970s the emergence of digital watches caused the collapse of no less than seventeen Swiss companies, and the traditional German clock industry slumped. When it was found that cash registers no longer needed mechanical moving parts, National Cash Register cut its workforce by a half. American Telephone and Telegraph reduced its workforce from 39,200 to 19,000 over a few years, and analogous economic structural changes were experienced in banking and other sectors. Today levels of unemployment that would have been unacceptable a decade ago must be reckoned part of the price caused by improved productivity achieved through increased automation.

We are now seeing the impact of computer-based systems on professional, as well as traditional 'blue-collar', jobs. It has been known for some years that middle managers were sometimes under threat from the 'automation axe' (see, for example, *Computerworld*, 26 March 1984). And even computer jobs were not immune from the technological developments. *Computer Weekly* (3 March 1983) wondered if there was a future 'for the service engineer'; and, in the same vein, Chris Nayler (writing in *Computer Talk*, 27 February 1984) explores whether computer-based program generators will 'put you out of a job'. Similarly, Romberg and Thomas (1984) consider how computers can be used to produce more reliable software 'in less time with fewer people'.

One possible emerging scenario is where skilled tasks in the functional loops are increasingly performed by computer systems, and one reason for this trend is clear – there are not enough human specialists to meet commercial and industrial needs in a cost-effective way. One observer (Sweet, 1987) comments: 'One of the prime reasons for the swing towards 4GLs is the huge applications backlog. . .'; and this is coupled with 'the chronic problems of finding enough skilled staff'. A solution to this problem may be a 4GL 'which will usually allow someone of *a lower skill level* than a traditional programmer to produce reasonable programming solutions in a fairly short space of time' (my italics). Progressive de-skilling is thus another consequence of computer developments that are facilitating a gradual closing of the functional loops.

We can discern a developing situation in which human beings are being pushed to acquire new skills under the growing pressure of evolving automatic systems, struggling to find new areas not yet occupied by software systems that are gaining in competence by the month. This is not the *current* situation but the seeds of such a scenario are manifest. All the functional loops are subject to the same broad analysis: we can envisage a progressive closing of the loops by means of a growing array of software systems of ever improving competence.

Software systems, in this changing situation, will increasingly be required to adapt. Thus Liang and Jones (1987) propose that a DSS 'should be aware of how it is being used and, then, automatically adapt to the evolution of its users'. In such a context there is discussion of *self-evolving capabilities*, a *user-involved evolutionary design*, and an *evolution management system*. Again it is significant that software systems are increasingly expected to adapt competently in circumstances requiring traditional management skills. Considering one aspect of project control, Townsend (1987) can ask: 'Can project management be done only by experts who can manage people effectively, or *can the software tools now available beat humans at their own game?*' (my italics).

We may expect software systems, increasingly encapsulating AI, to progressively close the functional loops in such areas as medicine, education, company planning and government decision-making. For example, the Financial Times Business Information publication FINTECH 2, No. 95 (16 December 1987) considers how 'electronic experts' are helping in government. Similarly, Aaronson and Carroll (1987) discuss how automated 'help desk' consultants are being designed to help human clients. Here the protocols of advisory interactions between human beings and machines are being studied – to facilitate the effective automation of a range of consultant functions.

The evolving situation is one in which computers are adopting many tasks performed by people, but in which no human beings are supplanting machines in the real-world functional loops. There is a unidirectional momentum in this situation: the loops are being progressively closed by gradually excluding people as crucial system components. The reliability and security of software systems in the increasingly automated functional loops are obviously of prime importance to human beings, ever more reliant on computer systems, in society. Before considering this aspect in more detail it is worth profiling the gradual closing of the loops in three important areas – factory automation, financial operations and military systems. These examples illustrate what is happening in all functional areas.

FACTORY AUTOMATION

The automation of factories has long been on the agenda: techniques of mechanisation associated with mass production were introduced decades ago when it was realised – by industrialists such as Henry Ford and others – that automation could dramatically increase the productivity of factory workers. Manufacturing processes could be laid out in a systematic way to minimise the transport of materials, to restrict the activities of workers to well-defined productive labour, and to optimise the use of expensive production machinery.

The early industrialists, in the US and elsewhere, were influenced by the work design techniques advocated by the American engineer, Frederick Winslow Taylor. His approach – known as *Taylorism* or *scientific management* – relies upon breaking manufacturing processes into small steps which could be repeatedly performed using a few simple skills. Here use is made of work simplification, task specialisation and time-and-motion analysis to exploit employees and machines to best advantage. Workers are required to perform the same simple tasks, time after time, with no opportunity for initiative or creative activity of any sort.

The Taylorist approach has been criticised as depicting people as nothing more than machine-like units in a production process, but perhaps this is inevitable where human beings and machines are expected to function in a tight symbiosis for production purposes (we have already indicated the modern tendency to view human beings as system components in computer-based networks). The interpretation of people as mere elements in factory production is vividly portrayed in the 1926 film *Metropolis* which is not only influenced by contemporary modes of mechanisation but which exploits the now familiar idea of an artificial creation, a robot, that is superior to a human being. Thus the scientist/ magician Rotwang declares: 'I have created a machine in the image of man, that never tires or makes a mistake. . . . Now we have no further use for living workers.'

It is interesting to remember that the notion of machine

superiority in fact predates *Metropolis* by many years. We
encounter mythological robots in pre-Christian tales, and in
1872 Samuel Butler wrote in *Erewhon*: 'whenever precision is
required man flies to the machine at once, as far preferable to
himself. Our sum-engines never drop a figure, nor our looms a
stitch; the machine is brisk and active, when the man is
weary; it is clear-headed and collected, when the man is
stupid and dull; it needs no slumber, when man must sleep or
drop....' It is clear that ideas that are directly relevant to
closing the functional loops – particularly in connection with
industrial production – have a long history. However, only
with the technological innovations of the Computer Age have
such ideas been realised in a comprehensive fashion.

By the end of the 1970s much attention was being given to
the concept of factories that could function in a largely
autonomous way. Thus Ruzic (1978), at the US National
Space Institute, discusses the 'completely automated manufacturing plant' with particular reference to the McDonnell
Douglas parts fabrication facility in St Louis. He notes the
'sheer size and loneliness of it all' – two acres of machines
work alone, apart from 'only a few men who glance occasional-
ly at a control panel or sweep the cuttings'. In a similar spirit,
Astrop (1979) – in an article headed 'Factory of the future is
no place for man' – highlights Japanese plans to develop
unmanned factories. Today, with enhanced computer facilities, largely automatic fabrication plants are in operation in
various parts of the world.

The concept of factory automation necessarily suggests the
idea of an assembly line, a common industrial phenomenon
throughout much of the twentieth century. However, it is
important to remember that factory production activity
involves much more than the necessary tasks of materials
handling, materials shaping, assembly and the like. Today we
can identify a host of activities – all of them using computer-
based systems – that are essential to the task of manufacture.
Such activities include: market research, computer-aided
design, automatic draughting and plotting, production control, materials planning, measurements and testing, quality
control, automatic packaging and automated warehousing.

There is an obvious sense in which such activities are peripheral to the central manufacturing function: they are, at the same time, essential if the commercial objectives of manufacture are to be achieved.

We see a wide spectrum of different, though linked, activities that are all crucially involved in the broad task of factory production – from the initial formulation of the product concept through all the tasks of design and manufacture to the final procedures for product packaging and distribution. What is significant for the purposes of the present book is that all the constituent activities are being progressively:

– computerised;

– linked in networks.

This suggests that there is a developing *integrated automation* to achieve cost-effective manufacture. A number of developing technologies are contributing in this rapidly developing situation. We can highlight, for example, AI (artificial intelligence), FMS (flexible manufacturing systems) and data communications.

AI is now aiding factory production in many ways: we need only mention the increasing use of expert systems in resource planning, product inspection and design optimisation; and the provision of sensory capabilities (vision, touch, etc) in industrial robots. One of the best known expert systems is the R-1 configuration expert, dubbed Xcon when Digital Equipment Corporation took over development responsibility from Carnegie-Mellon University. The system, producing configuration specifications from customer orders, is now used to aid the design of about ninety per cent of all DEC VAX computers. Xcon is said to be saving DEC around $18 million a year in component production.

There is now a growing recognition that companies cannot afford to ignore the available AI options. Williamson (1987), for example, declares that 'The question of whether AI technology can work in manufacturing is no longer an issue'; and Mark Fox, president of Carnegie Group, is quoted ('We're past the point of proving the technology. We're now at the point of finding whether people are smart enough to get involved with it').

Increasing attention is also being given to how communications facilities can be developed to optimise the use of data in the factory environment. Research into such aspects as protocols and standardisation is intended to accelerate the trend towards systems integration that is evident in manufacturing and elsewhere. The development of Open Systems Interconnection (OSI) and the associated Manufacturing Automation Protocol (MAP)* has immense significance for the progressive integration of factory functions at all levels. We can envisage how, for example, data generated through computer-aided design will also be exploited to regulate materials requisitioning and the control of robots, machine tools and other fabrication equipment.

Similarly, packaging procedures, warehousing dispositions and other matters will also come to be regulated by the provision of data generated initially for other purposes. And the impact of MAP and other OSI-linked features in the manufacturing environment will increasingly be seen as analogous to what is happening in other commercial sectors. For example, there is obviously no point in laboriously transporting (or converting) data manually if the requirements can be met cost-effectively using computers and communications links. Such a consideration, and all the corollaries, will increasingly be found to apply to all types of functional loops, whatever their nature and in whatever commercial or industrial sector they are found.

The central point, for our purposes, is that there is – via increased computerisation and networking – a progressive closing of the functional loops, a progressive functional marginalisation of the human components in the man/ machine systems. The example of factory automation serves as a nice paradigm, but we can take equally impressive examples from other sectors. They all illustrate the import-

*See the NCC publications, *What is OSI?* and *What is MAP?* (both by Colin Pye, both published in 1988).

ance of software reliability and security in circumstances where we are increasingly dependent on computer systems.

FINANCE AND PROGRAMMED TRADING

The computerisation of financial operations, of one sort or another, is almost as old as electronic computers. Banking applications were among the first uses of commercial systems in the 1950s, and the role of computers in the business world has long been recognised. In the 1980s computer-based systems, often claiming an 'AI content', were able to carry out auditing functions, to offer taxation advice and to recommend corporate policy options. Today expert systems are busy analysing banking credit policies, evaluating investment portfolios and regulating the global distribution of funds (via EFT, electronic funds transfer).

There is widespread recognition that the financial and business sector is well suited to the progressive application of computer systems. For example, the 1987 Ovum report, *Expert Systems in Banking and Securities*, points out that 'the world's leading banks are all active in building artificial intelligence applications' and that 'some smaller banks are already involved'. Again the progressive closing of the functional loops, discerned in factory automation, is evident also in the financial sector.

We can chart how computerisation has progressively encroached upon the more difficult financial tasks. The early financial expert systems were expected to perform relatively simple operations. Such 'rear office' jobs as advising on letters of credit or supplying straightforward tax advice were computerised in the early-1980s, a further useful expansion of the role of business computers. At that time it was thought that such 'front office' tasks as insurance underwriting, securities trading and foreign exchange trading would not lend themselves to effective computerisation. Today, however, many of these tasks have been successfully automated, and we may expect progressive computerisation – particularly under the pressures of 1992 – in the years ahead. Such possibilities have been highlighted by the controversy surrounding the role of *program trading* in the 1987 financial collapse.

Doubts have been expressed for some years, not only with the benefits of hindsight, about the wisdom of allowing artificial systems to trade on the financial markets. Most of the 'expert systems' programmed to trade merely buy or sell, in a completely undiscriminating manner, when particular predefined market levels are reached. These are not true expert systems: they have no comprehensive domain knowledge base, and they would not be able to outperform even a novice human trader. Other systems are more discriminating but still fail to satisfy many sceptical observers.

A writer in *The Computer Law and Security Report* (May/June, 1987) considers particular legal issues raised by program trading. What happens, for example, if a holder of a large block of shares in a public company decides to sell the block in the hope that the quoted share price will then fall towards the standard trigger sell figure held in many expert systems? There is a legal dimension in this scenario that cannot be pursued here (the interested reader should follow up the above citation and the subsequent issue of the *Report*, July/August, 1987). For the purposes of the present book, it is enough to stress that computer-based systems are now securely entrenched in the global trading environments, not simply as convenient administrative tools but as influential decision-makers. Increasingly, human traders are forced to reckon with the behaviour of artificial systems in the financial markets.

It is significant that automatic program trading was thought by many observers to have been one of the main factors in the financial collapses of 1986 and 1987. The celebrated financial 'Big Bang' had encouraged trading on a global basis and had, in particular, given enhanced status to the expansion of automation that this demanded (we may expect the status of automation to be elevated again following what we may dub the 1992 Big Bang). *The Financial Guardian* (16 September 1986), for example, suggests that 'the principal reason that the US markets fell as far as they did was what is called program trading, by which computers decide on the basis of certain general market movements whether to buy or sell shares. . . .' On 26 October 1987 – a day soon dubbed 'Black Monday' – the New York stock-market computers recorded a massive spate of selling, involving 600 million transactions. This caused massive sales in London: the 274,000 computerised trade reports represented more than two and a half times the daily average.

It was quickly decided that much of the escalating sales volume on the various exchanges was caused by computer-based expert systems initiating sales at unprecedented levels. There were, however, to be some dissenters from the generally held opinion. Kull (1987), for example, in an article headed 'Wall Street kills the messenger', declared 'The barrelhead indictment of program trading systems in the stock market collapse was a classic public hoodwinking' and suggested that 'Once again, the computer was a scapegoat'. At the same time it is difficult to avoid the cautious view that program trading had at least had *some* impact: perhaps the only rational debate is about 'how much?'.

It is not necessary to *quantify* the impact of program trading to see that computers are now carrying out trading functions formerly performed by human beings. Just as computers have moved from 'rear office' to 'front office', so they are today carrying out trading tasks that, even a decade ago, would have been unthinkable. We are witnessing a progressive closing of the loops in the financial sector as we are in factory automation.

MILITARY SYSTEMS

Today computer-based systems are being used for many different types of military purposes. They assist in the fabrication of weapons components, they help to control tanks and aircraft, they guide torpedoes and missiles, they help to train personnel in the armed services, and they use 'gaming' and other techniques to model war scenarios. It is increasingly likely that computers will be key factors in both the starting and prosecution of wars: 'AI techniques will be exploited to give computers the power to decide on warfare and the ability to supervise the resulting war-making procedures. In the popular feature film *War Games*, human operators are effectively 'taken out of the loops'. This is a realistic depiction of what is happening today in various military systems, perhaps the most important area in which we can discern a closing of the functional loops.

Wars run by human generals are not the most welcome events to most people, and it is unlikely that wars run by computers will be much better. Here, above all, we need to have confidence in the reliability of our systems!

The potential competence of computers in initiating and prosecuting a war may seem obvious to some. A computer can process vast amounts of information more quickly than can any human being, and the accurate and speedy processing of information is essential to success in war. As, it is argued, a country with superior war-fighting computer will have an obvious strategic advantage, a notion that has occurred to politicians, generals and entrepreneurs in the United States and elsewhere. TRW Defense Systems (in California), for example, is aiming to develop computers that are as good as the best generals. TRW's Ed Taylor has observed: 'The main problem with fighting a modern war is that you have good generals and dumb generals'. The alternative is to program 'good' judgemental abilities into the computer, and to then let the machine run any ensuing conflict. One prediction is that the US armed forces will be using such computers in the mid-1990s.

However, before a war can be run it must be started, and we are not surprised to find that computers will be in at the beginning. Arthur C Clarke observed, as far back as 1982, that it is no longer true that wars begin in the minds of men – they could now start in the circuits of computers. He was envisaging what are now called *launch-on-warning* systems where computers receive information, decide that a country is under attack, and then launch a nuclear missile response – without consulting any human being! This is how the US Strategic Defence Initiative (SDI) system ('Star Wars') will be intended to operate. SDI, as exemplifying the most important functional loops likely to be developed on the planet, deserves to be considered in more detail (Chapter 7). Here we need only emphasise the significance of this emerging situation....

It seems likely that human beings will be increasingly excluded from the operational loops involved in war making: so computers, in this way, will be able to decide whether human life will continue on the planet. Again we need hardly emphasise the importance of reliable, secure software. We are well acquainted, in the years after Lockerbie, with what can happen when equipment is insufficiently secure; and the military arena offers potential hazard on a global scale. In January 1988 a Trident missile exploded on test over Cape Canaveral, an event that closely followed the publication of *A Handbook of Nuclear Accidents* (Peace Research Report No. 20, University of Bradford). This document is a sobering chronicle of nuclear near-misses. For example, a Titan II nuclear ballistic missile wrongly switched into a real launching sequence (human operators, still in the loop, were able to switch off the power supply). Another case involved the near launch of a Minuteman missile from its silo in Wyoming (the crew placed an armoured car on top of the silo to disrupt a possible launch). Again the importance of reliable, secure systems is obvious.

SUMMARY

This chapter – as a prelude to considering system reliability, system security and related topics – has emphasised the increasingly ubiquitous character of computer-based systems and has indicated how the effective functional loops are being closed (ie how human beings are being progressively marginalised in important real-world networks). The corollary is that there is an effective transfer of decision-making discretion from people to machines; and that, in consequence, the reliability and security of computer-based facilities are of growing importance.

It is easy to see why computers, in appropriate applications, are popular with politicians, managers, entrepreneurs and generals. Computers are adept at monitoring and control, and their speed of response offers clear advantages in dynamic competitive situations. This suggests that there will continue to be powerful pressures for comprehensive computerisation in all social sectors. Increasingly, our safety and security, the quality of our lives, will be in the hands of computer-based systems. Assuming that the systems are regulated ethically within the terms of political legitimacy – and this aspect too could be massively debated elsewhere – it is essential that we make our systems as reliable and secure as possible.

2 System Reliability

INTRODUCTION

The need for *reliable* computer systems is paramount, particularly in circumstances where we are depending more and more on automated facilities and where computer failure can threaten human life. But system reliability is often difficult to achieve: even small systems can present unexpected problems; and, whereas there is no tight correlation between system size and the likelihood of failure, large networked systems do tend to present their own characteristic problems. Computer systems, of whatever size, are complex entities, and there are many ways in which they may fail to meet requirements.

This chapter is concerned with *inadvertent* flaws in systems; the possibility of system failure caused by errors that have been *maliciously* introduced (ie the possibility of sabotage) is considered in Chapters 3 to 5. Preventive measures do of course often overlap the two categories. For example, a coding check that detects an error may be quite indifferent to how the error was introduced.

We can never assume – once systems are designed, hardware built and programs coded – that no mistakes have been made, that the specifications have been adequately defined, and that the requirements in the (possibly imperfect) specifications have been met. It is always necessary to check the designs, to test the hardware and software, to verify, to validate – according to carefully formalised procedures (that may themselves have serious shortcomings).

We *can* assume that designs will be imperfect and that there will be flaws in the practical realisation of the theoretical constructs. The systems may still be successful, but only if proper attention is paid to systems quality.

It has been suggested, perhaps mischievously, that the longest program that can be written correctly without the need for subsequent debugging comprises only five or six lines of code. Whether this is true or not, the point is made. It is all too easy for programmers to generate flawed systems, either because the original analysis was unsound or because of problems with program concepts and coding.

We often read accounts in the technical literature of where new systems have been released onto the market prematurely, usually because of commercial pressure. Bugs have been found in software and modifications are demanded. Even a typical video game – a small system – needs to be copiously checked before being released for sale, and here we may be talking about a few hundred lines of code (compare with the SDI software, expected to contain upwards of ten million lines written by thousands of different programmers – see Chapter 7).

Software needs to be tested as thoroughly as possible before it can be regarded as satisfactory, and even then it is wise to reach only tentative conclusions. Further system design flaws and coding errors may be found when the software begins performing in the real world. The sheer complexity of software systems, the fuzzy nature of much of the relevant theory, human fallibility and the problems of co-ordinating many people on even a relatively simple project all conspire to make software development an error-prone endeavour. The aim should always be to detect and remove as many software errors as possible without assuming that there may not be more bugs lurking in some dark corner.

Many approaches – some formal, some empirical – are now being developed to aid the software testing task. The Software Productivity Consortium (SPC) is encouraging the development of effective testing procedures and other mechanisms essential to the various life-cycle phases. SPC, with prestigious founder members – Boeing, Lockheed, Ford Aerospace and Communications, GTE Government Systems, McDonnell Douglas, United Technologies and TRW – was set up in 1984 to address the rapidly escalating software development costs. Work on standards and on developing formalised methods for evaluating software quality is also relevant to the design and construction of reliable systems.

The effective testing of systems faces many problems. What has been shown to be an excellent testing methodology with small systems may be totally inapplicable with large ones (it may, for example, be impossible to run through the full spectrum of checks that are theoretically demanded). Sometimes, as with many military systems, we cannot test by observing performance in the intended real-world conditions: we cannot launch an array of primed nuclear missiles simply to test the software (here 'success' or 'failure' would equally entail disaster). What often happens in systems testing is that there is a trade-off between practicality and thoroughness, with the implication that the testing task is never complete. Again we can emphasise the tentative nature of conclusions regarding the reliability ('correctness', 'accuracy', 'validity', etc) of computer systems.

This chapter briefly profiles, under separate heads, the spectrum of possible computer faults, key criteria that relate to system quality, aspects of quality assurance and testing, organisational strategies, and future trends. The main point is that computer systems, as highly complex functional entities, cannot be guaranteed to operate flawlessly in all circumstances. This is a serious matter in a world increasingly reliant on automation.

COMPUTER FAULTS

Classification

There are many ways in which faults can occur in computer systems, and various fault-classification schemes have been developed (see, for example, Martin, 1973; and Yourdon, 1972). Gibbons (1976) considers six basic types:

- inadequate input validation;
- design miscalculation;
- system control faults;
- hardware faults;
- software faults;
- human mistakes.

This implies that faults are invariably inadvertent, unintentional, unpredictable. For our purposes it is worth emphasising that faults in computer systems can be mischievous, alarmingly intentional, and predictable – at least by the perpetrator (see Chapters 4 and 5).

Inadequate Input Validation

All the required features of the system should be defined in the initial specification. This includes defining the types and ranges of input that the system is expected to handle. The system should be capable of detecting and rejecting all instances of 'illegal' data (bad data can, for example, corrupt the data base and cause the system to break down completely). In general, systems have little difficulty in detecting the simpler types of error (wrongly keyed characters, missing transactions, etc), but problems can arise with the more subtle types of input error. Mischievous individuals sometimes devise ways of circumventing the inbuilt system checks – with results that can be at best embarrassing for the system users, at worst catastrophic.

Design Faults

A principal consideration in system design is to enable the system to cope with exceptional operating conditions. For example, some peak loads are predictable whereas others are unexpected. The processing power and storage capacity of the system should be able to handle such variations without breakdown, even if there are delays before normal service is resumed (a poorly designed system may never catch up). If there are *gross* design faults, the system may collapse even under conditions of normal operation.

System Control Faults

The operational control of the computer system is often the joint responsibility of the inbuilt operating system and the user's own control software, either of which may be faulty. In such a case the consequences may be poor task scheduling, poor storage management and deadlocks. The system may operate satisfactorily for a time until faults in the design of a control facility introduce unacceptable delays or cause the system to 'seize up' completely.

Hardware Faults

Any of the physical components of a computer system may develop a fault, although today high levels of hardware reliability are to be expected. Integrated circuits, for example, are highly reliable in normal operating conditions; and, where the conditions are particularly arduous, efforts are made to take this into account in design (for example, systems expected to encounter high temperatures, sudden accelerations or high levels of radioactivity should be designed appropriately).

Program Faults

Faults can be introduced into computer programs in many ways, at any stage of the development life cycle. Program 'bugs' may be regarded as one of the most common causes of system failure. They are easily introduced into systems, and detecting and correcting them invariably occupy a substantial proportion of the system development time. Developers usually appear to proceed on the assumption that hardware is trustworthy but software needs extensive checks to ensure maximum reliability. Discussion of system 'correctness', quality assurance, system reliability, etc is massively concerned with software. (At the same time we should remember that considerable investment effort is being put into hardware development, mainly by the supplier companies.)

Software errors can be introduced at any, some or all of the development phases; for example:

- **in the requirements specification**. The analyst may have failed to specify how the system should behave in certain relevant circumstances, and the programmer may not notice the omission. In consequence the program may behave badly or, at certain times, fail to act at all;

- **in the system design**. The designer may choose the wrong algorithms or make other unsound theoretical assumptions. In such circumstances the subsequent program is sure to contain errors;

- **in implementation**. The programmer, through carelessness or incompetence, may not code what is required. Even a highly competent programmer is bound to make errors from time to time;

- **in maintenance**. When a program is being corrected or expanded, new faults may be introduced (and this in fact may be an unavoidable consequence). Thus Barr and Feigenbaum, in their prestigious *Handbook of Artificial Intelligence* (1981, Volume 1, p 149), observe that 'in order to modify a large system successfully, the programmer must understand the interactions of all its pieces, which can become an impossibly difficult task'. Similarly, Gibbons (1976) comments that 'the faults in some large operating systems and data management packages are numbered in thousands, and the number increases with time rather than diminishes'.

Other Human Mistakes

There are also many other ways in which human error can adversely affect the reliability of computer programs. The wrong versions of files and programs may be used; there may be incorrect responses to console messages; files may be wrongly purged or programs wrongly aborted; data media may be damaged by careless handling; etc.

It is obvious that there are many ways in which faults can be introduced into computer systems, and that such faults can cause poor system performance or total system collapse (see also Chapter 6).

QUALITY CRITERIA, MEASURES

It is obviously desirable that computer systems be of 'good quality' – though there is debate as to how such 'goodness' or 'correctedness' can be defined, recognised and ensured. At one level it is easy to see that computer systems should be reliable, and that various factors can contribute to this requirement. Gibbons (1976) highlights:

- **availability**, measured by such quantifiable features as mean time before failure (MTBF) and mean time to repair (MTTR). Here availability ('the proportion of the total time scheduled for operation that the system is actually available for normal service') can be represented as

$$(MTBF)/MTBF + MTTR$$

  It should be appreciated that a quantified availability does not in fact indicate unambiguously the mode of behaviour of the system: different patterns of failure can yield the same availability;

- **graceful degradation**, in which a system can limp along even though some components have failed. This mode of operation is likely to be preferable to total system collapse (see also Fault Tolerance, below);

- **fail-safety**, in which potentially catastrophic events are not allowed to happen;

- **data integrity**, signifying the ability of a system to prevent errors in its database, to detect them if they are not prevented, and to correct them or confine their effects;

- **system integrity**, signifying the ability of a system to detect faults in its own operation, and to correct them or limit the damage they cause. For example, the system may choose to stop the operation of a faulty program before it affects other programs or corrupts the database;

- **recovery capability**, signifying how quickly and how economically the system can get out of difficulty.

The significance of these various factors varies according to the type of computer system, the applications that it is intended to perform, the projected life of the application, etc. It is obvious that large, complex systems are more likely to present problems than small simple ones, but different types of programs of similar sizes may present very different types of difficulties. It is necessary, for example, to consider what is meant by the term 'software quality'.

Different authors highlight different (but usually overlapping) groups of qualities that are relevant to any determination of software quality (see, for instance, Cho, 1980; Reiffer, 1982). Here we encounter such qualities as reliability, efficiency, maintainability, consistency, testability, portability, etc – though such terms themselves usually require further elucidation. Myers (1976) defines 'software goals' (within a group of product objectives):

> User Definition, Functional Objectives, Publications (eg Documentation), Efficiency, Compatibility, Security, Service-ability, Installation and Reliability.

After surveying these approaches Macro and Buxton (1987), aiming to identify 'essential issues', suggest an approach to software quality and to how this might be achieved. For example, emphasis is given to the critical character of a) the compliance of a software system to the requirements expressed in the functional specification, and b) the modifiability of the system for maintenance and new versions. Reliability is seen as comprising aspects of the two.

It is further emphasised that high quality is not achieved as an event but as a process involving the major life-cycle steps (the outcome from each step 'should have its quality demonstrated as well as possible'). Moreover the requirement of system quality demands that the process be verified and that the software system be validated and certified. The tasks of verification, validation and certification (sometimes known as VV&C) can be defined:

Verification: the objective determination that the software development process has been satisfactory up to the point at which the implementation team declare that the system is compliant on the basis of their own tests.

Validation: the objective determination that the mandatory criteria of compliance and modifiability have been achieved. This involves testing the software and its documentation.

Certification: the objective determination that the system operates successfully in its working environment for a specified period (say, three or six months).

VV&C may be regarded as part of the quality process which itself may be defined in terms of Quality Control (QC), Inspection (QI) and Assurance (QA):

QC: the activities of an internal team who aim to ensure the quality of work at the various life-cycle stages. QC normally ends after independent verification but may resume when validation reveals defects in the software or documentation and backtracking up the life-cycle is necessary.

QI: independent verification of the software development process.

QA: independent determination of whether mandatory criteria for software quality have been met (see also QA, Testing, below).

A key objective is to achieve 'correct' software, though, as we may suspect, 'correctness' can be interpreted in various ways. Thus Abbott (1986) points out:

A computer system may be correct in a variety of ways. It may be correct in an abstract sense, ie the system may be in some way *inherently perfect*. It may be correct in the sense that it is a *perfect reflection of its user's expectations*. Or it may be technically or contractually correct, ie *it functions in accordance with the expressed specified wishes of its users*. (original italics)

The user is likely to be most interested in whether the system specification reflects the user's wishes, and in whether the system functions as specified. Both considerations are crucial in determining whether the system functions as intended in a practical real-world situation. Watts (1987) emphasises that concepts that have been used in other quality fields for a considerable time are now being introduced into the field of software quality. 'Software metrics' has been developed, with this consideration in mind, by such workers as McCall (1980), Perlis et al (1981) and Gilt (1987). Watts (1987) considers the features of a 'good' quality measure:

A quality measure must:

- provide the connection between the quality characteristic (or attribute) and the product properties constituting that characteristic;

- react sensitively to different degrees of the quality characteristic to be measured;

- guarantee that it will provide objective determination of the quality characteristic and of the mapping of the results onto a suitable judgement scale.

There appear to be seven criteria of 'goodness' which quality measures have to meet:

Objectivity: the measuring results obtained must be free from any subjective influences. It must not matter who the measurer is.

Reliability: a quality measure should secure stable and precise results however often the tests are carried out (assuming the conditions are comparable).

Validity: it is no use carrying out the test unless the measure really measures the correct characteristic.

Standardisation: there has to be a scale for unambiguous representation and comparison of the results.

Comparability: we need to know enough about the measure to allow us to compare it with other measures which claim to measure the same characteristic.

Economy: it is obviously desirable that the determination and evaluation of measuring values should involve as low cost as possible. This is obviously a matter of judgement: how does one ever determine how much quality is worth? All in all a simpler (cheaper) measure (even if it is slightly less accurate) is more likely to be used than a complicated (expensive) one.

Usefulness: a quality measure must satisfy a practical need. We add this rider to attempt to prevent people from measuring things which *can* be measured even though the results are not important to them.

QUALITY ASSURANCE, TESTING

In the early days of computing (when, incidentally, programming – as a supposed clerical job – was often left to women!), it was often assumed that programs could be guaranteed to be right at the first attempt. Soon, however, the need for program testing became all too obvious. In due course, as systems became more complex, the testing provision evolved into what became known as 'life-cycle quality assurance' – an approach requiring that the system be made correct at the beginning of development and kept correct from then on. Abbott (1986) describes aspects of quality assurance during analysis and design, for module testing, for integration testing, and for system testing.

A key purpose is to 'prove' the software, but it is emphasised, by Abbott and others, that *absolute* proof can never be achieved in this field. The most that can be claimed is that the software is the best that can be managed within the limits of available technical competence and project costs. Trade-offs are inevitable, though sometimes alarming when potential system failure represents a threat to human life (see Chapters 6 and 7).

The realistic (but modest) ambition that software be rendered as good as possible reminds us that software development is a difficult task, error-prone and fraught with hazard. Chantler (1981) – in distinguishing between *possible, probable* and *absolute* correctness – has emphasised that no amount of testing can improve a program, and that only *probable* correctness can be accomplished. (We may find it less than reassuring to learn that the software controlling an intensive care unit, an air traffic control system or a nuclear missile complex is only *probably* correct!)

Various strategies can be adopted, however, to maximise the beneficial effects of testing. One approach is to test the components of a program progressively, during development, relying on program components that have already been proved (albeit only to a level of probability) to be correct. One theoretically attractive, though costly, option is to develop a purpose-built *test harness* for each component that needs to be tested (more economically, a 'universal' test harness, able to accommodate a range of components, may be possible).

Software can be developed in a hierarchical fashion where program components are functionally defined with well defined data interfaces – an approach that is seen as generating software with 'self-testing' features. Chantler (1981) has noted that the decision to adopt such a self-testing approach 'will necessarily affect the order in which program components are developed'. This suggests that consideration of testing strategy is bound to affect the approach to system design. Thus software design activity can be influenced by tasks (eg involving testing and maintenance) that are normally represented as taking place at later stages in the system development life cycle.

Many different test methods are being developed as important features in software engineering. Traditional testing methods are sometimes dubbed 'ad hoc' by modern theorists with a more rigorous approach. Today attention is being given to such aspects as *functional* testing and *structure* testing: functional testing can be used in connection with the generation of test cases, derived from analysis of the software specification, appropriate to a particular 'level of abstraction' (one problem is to decide 'at what level of abstraction to test' – Abbott).

The various ad hoc and functional test methods exhibit 'black box' features: the software is effectively *closed* to the tester. By contrast, structure methods use 'white box' (or *open*) testing, and knowledge of the software can suggest ways of organising effective test tactics. Abbott (1986, Chapter 7) discusses various approaches to structure testing (statement testing, branch testing, LCSAJ testing, etc).

When the tests have revealed program errors, debugging can take place, ie the faults can be removed to improve the program. It is then prudent for fresh tests to be carried out to ensure that the amended program is sound. Thus debugging is regarded as identifying those areas of the program that cause performance errors and enabling the program to be changed as necessary. Error location is usually seen as the difficult part of the debugging task, with correcting a coding error a more straightforward operation.

However, it *is* possible that debugging will reveal a fundamental design error – in which the necessary modifications, involving backtracking through the development life cycle, will be costly. (To avoid such expensive iterations, systems designers generally aim to produce individual units that are logically and functionally independent.) And it is also possible, as already mentioned, that program changes – as part of debugging or as part of a system enhancement – may have unexpected adverse consequences elsewhere in the system.

One testing approach is to exploit the test results generated from specified test cases. With such information – and a knowledge of the code – it should be possible to determine the source of the error. Here the programmer is advised to approach code in a sceptical manner, to carry out what one observer (Sommerville, 1985) calls a 'thought' execution of the code, rather than approaching the code as if they know what it does (and so subconsciously reading it as if it does what was intended). When code inspection fails to detect errors whose presence is suspected, it may be necessary to use, for example, program statements that produce data values at appropriate places in the program. This, though sometimes useful, can be a time-consuming process. It is important that, once the program is delivered, any diagnostic outputs formerly used for debugging purpose are inhibited. A growing range of debugging aids is now available, with innovatory commercial products frequently described in the technical literature.

The growth in the provision of debugging measures extends beyond the provision of technical methodologies: organisational changes are sometimes necessary. One approach is to establish independent quality assurance (QA) departments designed to operate separately from the project developers. A key aim here is to circumvent the special interests of developers who may be expected to test their own products. Some US organisations have created 'adversary teams' (modelled on the 'black teams' that once operated in some IBM divisions). Macro and Buxton (1987) distinguish between 'benevolent' (author-level) testing of software and 'adversarial' testing (by independents).

Adversary teams (like other test groups) can use a variety of debugging aids. Some have already been cited, and mention can also be made of profiler programs that insert software probes into a program to monitor which parts are executed by test data (whereupon dedicated tests can be organised), and mutation systems where artificial errors are introduced into a program under test and the resultant mutant program fed with test data. It has been suggested that adversary teams can sometimes offer a home to skilled but recalcitrant individuals (for example, free-wheeling hackers) who may otherwise be an embarrassment to a company. The main purpose of an adversary team (including, for instance, dissident nonconformists, PhD loners, etc) is to make software systems crash: a successful test is one that causes a system to fail. This is also the aim of what have been called 'bug bounty hunters', independent operators called in to detect bugs (and paid by results). Thus the adversary teams may be depicted as malicious, and bounty hunters as mercenary.

THE FUTURE

We have emphasised the growing range of testing facilities available to system developers. It is inevitable that new aids, increasingly automated (and having 'AI content'), will continue to appear in the future. Abbott (1986) describes 'a number of validation techniques which have not yet matured to the extent necessary for everyday commercial use'. Attention is given to:

- **symbolic evaluation**, involving the use of a software package, a symbolic evaluator, to 'interpret' the source code of software and to deduce the input necessary to produce a required output or the output that will be produced from a given input. This approach, developed for use in the validation of complex mathematical routines, has yielded various techniques (eg partition analysis);

- **partition analysis**, where symbolic evaluation is used to reduce a program and its specification to a common abstract form so that they may be directly compared. A global symbolic evaluator is employed to enumerate the computations carried out on all paths through the program and the 'datasets' used by every path. The process produces partition analyses representing the program and its specification: the analyses can then be compared to determine whether the program fulfils the specification;

- **domain testing**, intended to determine a set of test data that will bring 'domain' and boundary errors to light. The program is analysed by means of mathematical methods using hypergeometry. The few published papers on this technique 'have the distinction of being, to the layman, amongst the least comprehensible ever written' – Abbott;

- **program mutation**, already mentioned, is a method of evaluating the thoroughness and completeness of testing. The system operates like an interactive test harness but is also able to generate mutant programs and to test those too. It is sometimes emphasised that 'mutation', in this context, does not always involve the introduction of errors: the program changes are often 'benign';

- **static analysis**, which has traditionally involved deducing the existence of errors in software simply by analysing its source code. Analysers, in this context, may be concerned with procedures flow or data flow, and a further (newer) type is interested in information flow. Here use is made of 'cause-effect graphing' to show what data is used in producing what results;

— **formal verification**, exploiting 'invariant assertions' to prove the program in a stepwise fashion, each step seeking to prove that the assertions following a segment of code hold, assuming the assertions preceding the segment to be true. Efforts are being made to automate what is otherwise a laborious process, though it is perceived that there are disadvantages in *full* automation;

— **test monitoring**, where the execution of tests is monitored and the use detected of non-distinct values for variables. It is assumed that only where two variables share a common value is detection of an error impossible. The emphasis is on ensuring that the distinct values rule is properly applied. Monitors could be produced to detect boundary errors and to 'snapshot' the data at strategic points in procedural flow.

Such techniques – all showing promise, though to varying extents – are all receiving attention in the literature and elsewhere. They herald advances in system testing that will be increasingly important in an automated world in which the functional loops are being progressively closed. Such advances will aim to identify the appropriate information for use in testing, to determine how best to interpret the information, and – as far as possible – to exploit automated methods at every stage of the process.

The increased use of automation in testing software systems does of course suggest a variant on the ancient concern expressed by *quis custodiet ipsos custodes*? We may ask – who will test the testers?

SUMMARY

This chapter has emphasised the importance of reliable computer systems, particular in circumstances where computer failure can threaten human life. It is emphasised that here we are concerned with *inadvertent* faults in systems, flaws that exist despite all good intentions. A little has been said about computer faults in general (including flaws in input data and hardware failure), but the emphasis has been on software systems flaws and on how these can be detected with a view to making program changes.

Attention has been given to what counts as 'goodness' or 'correctness' in a program. Features that serve as quality criteria have been highlighted, and the VV&C (verification, validation and certification) framework is outlined. Principal quality concerns – Quality Control, Quality Inspection and Quality Assurance – are profiled, with brief reference to software metrics and to what can serve as effective measures of quality.

Aspects of testing are surveyed, with focus on whether (and to what extent) software can be proved – we find that we can never be absolutely sure that software systems do not contain flaws. The debugging requirement is briefly discussed and mention is made of specific approaches to testing. Finally, following Abbott (1986), a number of validation techniques that are being discussed today and that are likely to bear fruit tomorrow are indicated. Emphasis is given to the likelihood of increased automation in software system testing, and we wonder how the soundness of the automated techniques will themselves be ascertained.

A principal message – which (in view of Chapters 6 and 7) is worth repeating – is that a degree of uncertainty necessarily attends the testing process, however it is conducted, at every stage of the system development life cycle. Our conclusions about software correctness must always be tentative. It is important to remember this in circumstances in which human life is increasingly dependent upon the proper functioning of automated systems.

3 Computer Security

INTRODUCTION

Computer security covers a multitude of topics: every aspect of the computer installation should be considered from the security viewpoint – to neglect any aspect is to render the installation vulnerable to accidental or deliberate threat. It is necessary to appreciate the range of hazards that can threaten effective computer operation, to be aware of typical computer-linked disasters that have occurred in the real world, and to appreciate the general approach to security that can minimize risk.

This chapter profiles the threat spectrum and discusses security principles, risk management and other important security questions. The individual computer security aspects – relating to hardware, software, people, contingency, etc – are considered, and emphasis given to the importance of good security for modern computer installations and other computer-based facilities. Topics such as insurance and fault tolerance computing are briefly considered, and we even encounter a security robot – a singular herald of things to come.

The possibility of mischievous or malicious threats to computer security is also mentioned but treated in greater detail in Chapters 4 and 5. Today *intentional* breaches of computer security – involving, for example, hackers and 'viruses' – are hot topics in both the general and technical literature. But the fascination that such phenomena arouse should not be allowed to detract from the more traditional, more routine aspects of computer security. A fire or an earthquake is likely to do much more damage to a computer installation than even the most determined hacker or virus maker.

The environments in which computer security needs to be addressed are constantly changing, sometimes seeing a progressive evolution with technological development and sometimes seeing rapid shifts when new legislation or financial innovations are introduced. Many complementary technologies – solid-state fabrication, optic fibres, laser systems, sensor technology, robotics, etc – bear directly on the security question, as do the increased levels of networking in the modern world, the shifting military and political alliances, and the evolving role of human beings in the man/machine symbiosis. Data protection legislation – for example, the UK Data Protection Act 1984 – has vast implications for security*, as does the progressive deregulation (in financial trading) that was involved in the 1986 'Big Bang' and that will feature in the upheavals of 1992. The 1984 Act requires all data users to observe the principles set out in Schedule 1. The Eighth Principle places an obligation on computer bureaux and data users:

> 'Appropriate security measures shall be taken against unauthorised access to, or alteration, disclosure or destruction of personal data and against accidental loss or destruction of personal data.'

This serves to emphasise that companies, in the UK and elsewhere, are legally obligated to maximise the security of their computer-based facilities in various regards. Legislation apart from that involved in data protection is also relevant (but cannot be explored here). And it should be emphasised that there are many other pressures on the managers of computer systems that encourage them to scrutinise security questions: for example, they are likely to be interested in profitability and commercial success. Thus Drysdale (1988) cites the case of an irate customer calling an equipment

*See, for example, *Security and the 1984 Data Protection Act*, NCC Publications with DTI support, 1987

supplier to complain about the loss of $5000 worth of spreadsheet development (an event 'likely caused by a lack of security ... ').

This chapter profiles the main areas that should be considered in relation to the security of computer-based systems. The topic is a vast one, and the chapter is intended to give no more than a flavour. It serves the general purpose of the present book – to emphasise the need for reliable and secure computer systems in a world that is increasingly dependent upon automated processes.

THE THREAT SPECTRUM

The multifaceted nature of computer security has already been stressed. It is worth emphasising also that the complete spectrum of computer systems – from the most modest micro to the largest international network – are potentially at risk.

The investigative journalist Duncan Campbell (1989), in an engaging article ('Keep your secrets'), examines the spectrum of threats to the security of data held on a simple personal computer. He emphasises that there are no 'absolutes' in the security business, that the best that can be achieved is 'low risk' rather than 'no risk' at all. Then attention is given to encryption and other security provisions, and to the efforts of US and British agencies to further expand their global electronic surveillance capabilities. This suggests again what we saw in Chapter 1, that there is a dimension to computer security that is massively political – and we cannot explore that part in the present book. It is enough here to remark that just as the humble micro is not secure, so neither is the large data communications network (whether the threat is posed by freelance hackers, industrial spies or official agencies).

Today there is growing pressure in the United States to develop a revolutionary 'superhighway' that would transform data transmission. By 1989 Senator Gore of Tennessee had laid legislation before Congress, proposing government funds for development of the network. The fibre-optic system would have a capacity of three gigabits, the performance equivalent of transmitting about 500 average-length novels a second.

Again the security problem is paramount.

The fibre-optic cables that would carry the data would be vulnerable to breaks, data interception and tapping. This is a problem that has not yet been fully addressed, though – with the project being supported by IBM, political leaders, universities, etc – it seems likely that the network will be implemented.

The point is a simple one: security is a complex problem that threatens computer systems of every size, whether they are networked or not, and whatever the real-world applications to which they are devoted. Before considering security principles, the question of risk and the main security aspects, it is worth glancing at some typical computer disasters that have occurred in recent years.

SOME DISASTERS

Disasters that have afflicted computer installations and other computer-based facilities are frequently reported in the computer literature (the more spectacular events often make it to the popular press). Thus Hewitt (1988) reports a fire at a major Hewlett Packard site that destroyed a computer system and left the computer room covered in ash, dust and water. An HP 3000 Series 52 and peripherals were destroyed at the Immingham-based shipping company, the Exxtor Group. The Birmingham-based Computer Disaster Recovery supplied a back-up machine within 24 hours of the disaster, but Exxtor has still lost about 25% of its processing capacity. In its seven-year existence, Computer Disaster Recovery has attended about two dozen disasters, including a firebomb attack, a flooded computer room and a Frankfurt fire that destroyed a whole building.

Efforts have been made (though not, for example, by the UK government) to collect statistics on computer disasters. For example, the UK consultancy BIS Applied Systems produced a *Computer Disaster Casebook* in 1983 (with a second edition issued in 1987 and a further update in October 1988). This publication offers a statistical overview of disaster cases collected from 1965 (half the reported cases have occurred in the last three years), provides case histories (date, company, equipment, incident details, etc), and includes an index by type of disaster. Thus Figure 3.1 shows disaster statistics for 1983 and 1987. It is significant that software-linked disasters have shown the largest increase in types of

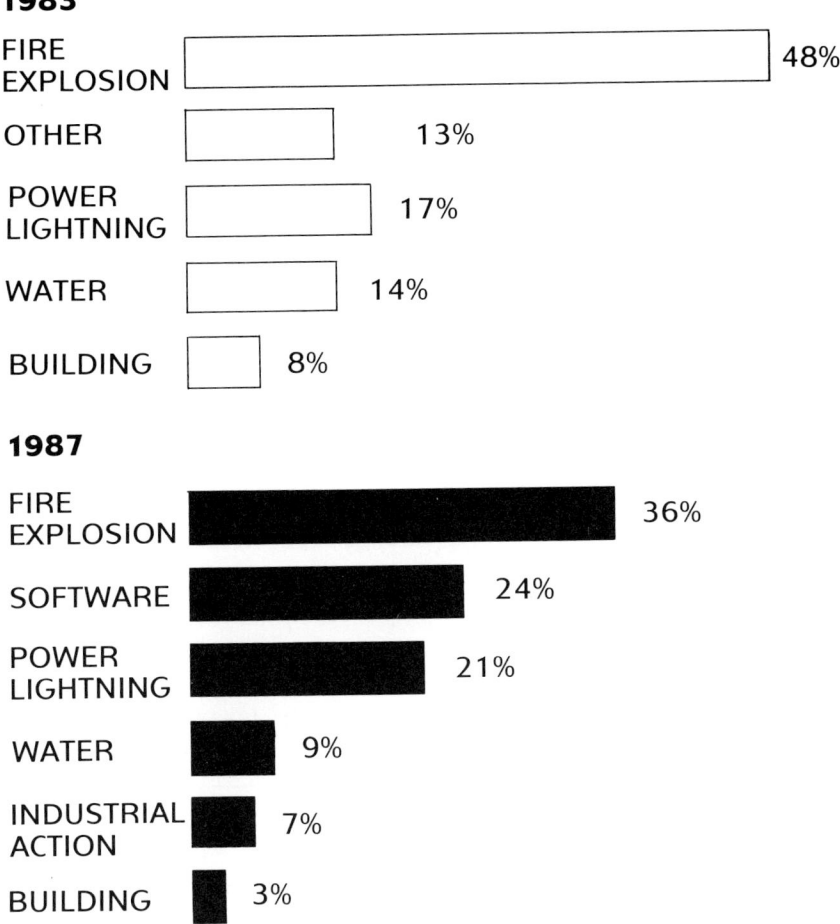

1983

FIRE EXPLOSION — 48%
OTHER — 13%
POWER LIGHTNING — 17%
WATER — 14%
BUILDING — 8%

1987

FIRE EXPLOSION — 36%
SOFTWARE — 24%
POWER LIGHTNING — 21%
WATER — 9%
INDUSTRIAL ACTION — 7%
BUILDING — 3%

Figure 3.1   Causes of Computer Disasters
Source: *Computer Disaster Casebook*, BIS Applied Systems, 1987
Permission Acknowledged

reported cases (as DP managers have increasingly been pushed to provide improved services using limited programming resources).

More than sixty instances of fire or explosion are recorded in the BIS casebook (with a quarter of the reported fires being caused by arson). Details of where and when the fires started and whether the installation was staffed are shown below:

During week	68%
Over weekend	32%
During day time	39%
During evening	13%
During night time	48%
Installation staffed	32%
Installation not staffed	68%
Started inside computer room	41%
Started outside computer room	59%

	Number of Cases	
Cost in £	Damage	Loss
0 – 1,000	16	13
1,001 – 10,000	7	6
10,001 – 100,000	20	14
100,001 – 250,000	10	7
250,001 – 500,000	6	7
500,001 – 1,000,000	3	7
1,000,001 – 5,000,000	1	5
over 5,000,001		4

Figure 3.2   Costs by Number of Disaster Cases
Source: *Computer Disaster Casebook*, BIS Applied Systems, 1987
Permission Acknowledged

As we may expect, the cost of disasters varies enormously according to the gravity of the events. BIS present the costs for damage and loss in the surveyed cases, though in some cases it was difficult to ascertain the full extent of business losses (see Figure 3.2).

We may also regard it as significant that the number of computer disasters surveyed is increasing, though this is hardly surprising in view of the rapidly expanding number of computer applications. Figure 3.2 gives a breakdown of when particular disasters, of various types, occurred.

Disaster	Year					
	60s	70s	80–82	83–84	85–87	Total
Fire Arson Explosion	3	18	18	11	13	63
Lightning Power	0	4	4	10	19	37
Water	1	7	4	0	3	15
Structure	0	1	1	1	3	6
Software	0	1	3	8	30	42
Industrial Action	0	2	0	5	6	13
Total	4	33	30	35	74	176

Figure 3.3   Numbers of Disasters by Type and Time
Source: *Computer Disaster Casebook*, BIS Applied Systems, 1987
Permission Acknowledged

It is worth glancing at a few of the disasters highlighted in the BIS casebook. The following examples, selected more or less at random, are abbreviated versions of the reported cases (none involving malice or mischief has been included – see Chapter 4):

In October 1965 a fire started on the premises of a textile

manufacturer. IBM equipment and accounting records were destroyed but the impact on the business was small since only one system had been computerised.

In July 1968 torrential rain followed by high tides caused the River Avon to overflow its banks and to flood the neighbouring Bristol area, resulting in the computer complex at the site of a tobacco manufacturer to be flooded waist high. Equipment was corroded and the computer was unserviceable. All the magnetic tapes were salvaged.

In 1975 the false ceiling in the computer room of an electronics company collapsed, causing the room to be covered with rubble. An efficient contingency plan was implemented but the computer room was out of action for six weeks and the air conditioning had to be fully recommissioned before the ICL 1906A computer could be powered up again.

In August 1977 a control equipment malfunction on the premises of a paper manufacturing company caused an eight-foot high boiler to explode. The boiler, weighing more than a ton was driven through the ceiling, up through the data preparation room and into the night sky before landing on an office twenty feet away. An ICL 2903 computer and all the data preparation terminals disappeared through a twenty foot square hole. The subsequent costs of back-up and other provisions were substantial.

In January 1979 cold weather caused a burst in premises over a Manchester accountants' office. The subsequent build-up of water caused a ceiling to collapse, severely damaging two VDUs and covering the computer in dirt. Subsequent costs amounted to around £11,000.

In September 1983 a fire occurred at the US Air Force Daws Hill base and the computer installation was burned out. It was thought that the fire was caused by a squirrel gnawing through the protective covering of power cables. (Squirrels have also been implicated in other disasters.) The damage to the site was around £500,000.

In June 1984 a fire was caused by a cigarette at an engineering facility and computer warehouse complex in Hounslow, Middlesex. One hundred firemen required more than three hours to bring the fire under control. Full recovery took six weeks to achieve – with losses estimated at £20 million of stock (mainframe computers, spare parts, etc).

In 1986 workmen moved furniture into an office above a computer room belonging to a multinational organisation. The floor began to buckle under the weight and then the ceiling of the computer room broke. Debris was scattered over the equipment. It was estimated that the disruption cost the company more than £3 million.

In January 1987 an electrical fault started a fire at the Royal Artillery's Larkhill Barracks, near Salisbury, Wilts. The unit was used to train soldiers to fire missiles at aircraft. An army spokesman said that the fire had damaged the unit's central computer.

APPROACHING SECURITY

It is obvious that the security question has to be approached simultaneously on many fronts, and that as much (if not more) attention needs to be given to basic traditional requirements as the new-fangled threats that may sometimes have a higher profile than they deserve. As one writer puts it, 'Forget danger posed by hackers and gropers. Worry about basic housekeeping first' (*Electronic Office*, 118, 30 November 1988). It is pointed out that security is currently a hot topic because of publicity 'about the horrors of computer viruses and the enormous amounts of money being lost to white-collar fraudsters who manipulate computer systems'. Graham Brown of Neaman Bond Associates is quoted: "Companies are more vulnerable to their own staff's stupidity than criminal activity."

The basic computer security requirements are clear enough: people expect computer systems 'to work properly and be available when required' (Wood, 1982). Ideally a system is designed to be secure against deliberate threat and inadvertent hazard. It may be emphasised that a computer system – hardware, software, media, etc – may be beautifully designed, well conceived as a reliably functioning unit. But what of the building, the human operators, the external environment? There are many dimensions of security, and any adequate security strategy will need to address them all. Moreover, whatever plans are formulated, whatever intelligent system designs are implemented, there will always be faults of one type or another, sooner or later, with greater or lesser effects. Then we need fault-tolerance provisions, contingency (back-up) plans, insurance and other protective devices. And it can be emphasised again that no measures can give *absolute* protection.

One approach is to tackle security on a modular basis, dealing with systems or environmental sectors in turn; or a hierarchical approach may be adopted. For example, various levels of protection can be given to a system according to its type and complexity:

- a small machine, or dedicated system with no resident files and no multiprogramming, can be protected by straightforward conventional methods;

- a system with resident files and an operating system that allows a stream of programs to be run serially may require special measures to offer protection from programs under test, malicious programmers, etc;

- with a multiprogramming system, the operating system must not only protect the resident files and itself, but must keep the programs from interfering with each other or violating each other's privacy;

- the necessary level of security is increased if the system is on-line, because the users and potential penetrators gain a degree of anonymity when working via a telecommunications line;

- the most stringent protective measures are required if the dial-up telephone network is involved because of its increased scope for gaining unauthorised access to the computer system.

In such different circumstances use can be made of dedicated security systems and security reviews (as effective hardware, software and methodologies designed to offer maximum system security). For example, Saari and Parker (1989), drawing on experiences in Finland and the United States, present a baseline methodology for reviewing security. The 'baseline concept' is described and seven computer security topics are identified for categorizing the baseline controls.

The key consideration behind the baseline concept is that virtually all well-run organisations use a well-known set of information security controls; and common use can serve as a guide when making decisions on controls. In this context the following topics were considered:

- manual assurance of data integrity;
- physical security;
- operations security;
- management-initiated controls;
- computer program development and maintenance;
- computer system control;
- computer system terminal access control.

The baseline controls were then refined; criteria for identifying a control were identicated; and an approach to assessing an organisation's security level against the baseline security is described. It is suggested that the proposed methodology is of great value because it gives 'more realistic and better justified information for top management to be able to make prudent decisions.'

There is a widespread perception that many security measures in companies and other organisations are often inadequate. Wood (1988), for example, comments on 'management dissatisfaction with information security.' One problem is that security provisions can rarely anticipate new modes of sophisticated threat ('viruses are but one of many new developments for which we in the community do not have effective and practical countermeasures'). At the same time it is possible to improve security provisions in the context of knowledge of likely threats.

It is suggested that, for example, there are cultural biases working against information security, that security models are 'woefully inadequate' (Wood, 1988), that mere lip service is paid to the economic desirability of good security, and that conditions of information overload ('infoglut') make it increasingly difficult to plan for effective security. Again, coherent methodologies are essential if such problems are to be overcome. A foundation for information security should be developed with focus on required policies and (technical and procedural) standards. Automated tools – risk analysis packages, spreadsheets, data dictionaries, project management packages, graphics packages, etc – can be used in the context of careful planning.

The main point is to recognise the multifaceted nature of the computer (or information) security problem. It is then essential to approach the system in a systematic way, in full awareness of the relevant methodological and automated tools that can aid the quest for good security. One key consideration is the assessment of risk. This is briefly discussed before we profile the other principal security topics.

RISK MANAGEMENT

Risk management, an important corporate need and responsibility, is the effective means whereby types (and levels) of threat are systematically evaluated and measures developed to counter them. An initial step is to identify all the elements, assets and resources (associated with the computer-based configuration) that could be at risk. One broad classification would include:

- **hardware**: central processor, disk drives, terminals, modems, physical storage facilities, etc;

- **software**: operating system, compilers, application programs, audit routines, back-up copies, etc;

- **data and media**: master files, input data, software

documentation, disk packs, etc;

- **communications**: telephone circuits, electronic mail, postal services, private data-carrying services, etc;

- **environment**: building structure, power supplies, cleaning services, local geology (eg proneness to earthquake), likelihood of terrorism, etc;

- **organisation**: management policy and structure, personnel aspects, etc;

- **support:** maintenance staff, auditors, consultants, delivery services, customers, etc.

Then it is necessary to identify the types of risk to which each of the above categories is subject. An initial approach might be to divide the task into *accidental* and *deliberate* risks. Such a division is virtually self-evident: *accidental* risks could derive from shortcomings in systems design, faulty components, poor architecture, human carelessness, extreme weather conditions, etc; *deliberate* risks could derive from sabotage, theft, espionage, industrial action, etc (all involving human intent).

The types of risk, interacting with the characteristic elements of the organisation, may produce a variety of losses. These can be identified as:

- **property losses**: damage, destruction, theft, pollution, etc;

- **liability losses**: breach of contract, copyright infringement, libel, slander, sedition, etc;

- **personnel losses**: death, illness, injury, deterioration, industrial action, resignation, leave of absence, etc;

- **financial losses**: bad debts, dishonest employees, etc;

- **business interruption losses**: delayed cash flows, rising prices, penalty clauses, etc.

It is now possible to quantify, on a probability basis, the losses that will be incurred over a particular period by a particular risk, ie it is feasible to offer a measurement of risk.

The *expected loss* is obtained by multiplying the mean value of the monetary loss that would result from an occurrence of the risk, by the frequency over unit time with which the risk is expected to occur. This procedure can help to establish the seriousness of a particular risk, and so suggest to managers a hierarchy of priorities for countermeasures. Then the cheapest countermeasures that will reduce the expected losses to a minimum can be sought. (At the same time, any important *non*financial criteria should be borne in mind.) The total expected costs are shown in Figure 3.1.

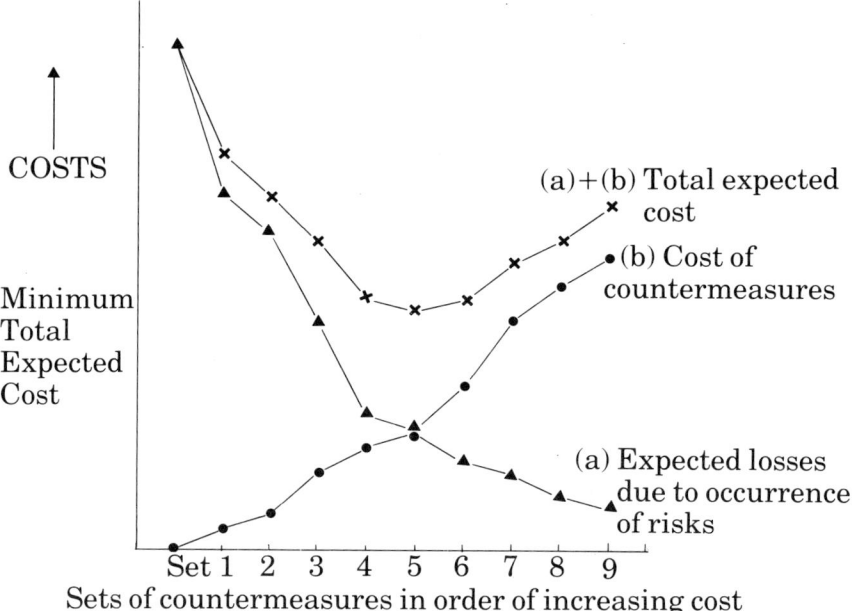

Figure 3.1   Relationship of Countermeasures and Costs

It should not be assumed that risks always have to be *avoided* by, for example, abandoning a service or implementing a set of effective countermeasures (which may be expensive). It is also possible to *accommodate* a risk (where its worst consequences would only be minor), to *reduce* a risk, and to *transfer* a risk (eg via insurance). Whatever risk strategy is adopted, it must be implemented systematically and comprehensively; and the risks and countermeasures should be constantly monitored – fluctuations in all the relevant quantified factors (probabilities, costs, etc) are to be expected. Moreover the entire security programme should be periodically reviewed to determine how well it is performing and what changes, if any, are required to maintain optimum performance.

PHYSICAL SECURITY

The physical environment, for security purposes, covers a multitude of topics. We are variously concerned with natural risks (from geology, meteorology, etc), the structural reliability of buildings (are they, for example, safe from 'neighbourhood risks'?), services (such as electrical power, fire prevention and air conditioning), access control (to exclude unauthorised individuals), and electromagnetic and other forms of radiation.

Many of the potential threats posed by the physical environment can be avoided by an intelligent approach at the planning and design stage of the installation. Risks can be sensibly avoided, or unavoidable risks neutralised by appropriate countermeasures. As an initial consideration, care should be taken in choosing the site for the computer installation. Attention should be given to the prospect of such natural phenomena as high winds, subsidence (ground settlement, collapse of mine workings, failure of culverts, etc), lightning (structural damage may be unlikely but power supplies can be affected), heavy snow, landslip, flooding and earthquakes.

Neighbourhood risks can derive from proximity to other (possibly high-risk) buildings, from transport facilities (that may cause collisions or the spillage of toxic materials), from a sudden break in the availability of public services, and from a range of sociopolitical risks (ranging from the activities of vandals, rioters, demonstrators, terrorists, etc on the one hand to nuclear war on the other). The architecture of the building may be expected to withstand most threats posed by natural hazard and human action. And it should also be remembered that current legislation – eg the Health and Safety at Work Act, the Factories Act, the Fire Precautions Act – imposed stringent requirements on building developments in the UK, just as there is analogous legislation in other countries.

Particular care should be taken to prevent fire and to control it (should it occur). The NCC author Mike Wood offers an excellent introduction to the multifaceted fire question in his 1986 book, *Fire Precautions in Computer Installations*, and offers useful advice in a further 1986 title, *Guidelines for Physical Computer Security*. Again the architecture of the building should include appropriate provisions for fire prevention, detection, quenching, etc.

Fire detection devices should be installed to protect all the necessary items of equipment and the rooms (and associated environs) in which they are situated. For example, protection should be afforded to:

- the central processor, disk packs, terminals, etc;
- floor and ceiling voids that carry cables;
- air conditioning ducts;
- the rooms in which computer equipment is housed and media stored.

It should also be remembered that fire detectors and fire-quenching equipment (eg sprinklers) can bring further problems. False alarms can occur and water released to quench a fire may damage computers, media, etc. Water carrying conductive sediments may cause short circuits, and sprinkler heads may be accidentally struck, causing water to be discharged onto fully powered equipment that is operating normally. Gas flooding systems are a fire control alternative, though with their own characteristic drawbacks. Portable fire extinguishers should also be provided.

Access control can be achieved using guards, mechanical locks, electronic systems and even robots (see Automated Security, below). Guards and other security personnel have all the obvious human shortcomings – proneness to fatigue, limited attention spans, corruptibility, etc. Mechanical locks may be inconvenient (if, for example, a person is carrying something), and problems may be caused if cards or keys are lost. Electronic push-button keyboards can offer a high level of access control but can sometimes be circumvented by ingenious villains.

Various points should be considered in choosing an access control system. For example, it is necessary to give attention to:

— the physical nature of the area to be controlled;

— what the area is to be used for;

— the value of the resources in the area;

— the frequency with which entry is required;

— the after-sales service provided by the supplier.

Such considerations, however, only relate to one type of access, that involving the ingress of people. But this is not the only type of access that can threaten the security of a computer installation. Information can be vulnerable to access by such means as:

— *bugging* (where detection/transmission devices have been infiltrated into the computer equipment;

— *wiretapping* which, like bugging, can occur at any point in the system where access can be obtained to processing modules or cables;

— *the monitoring of 'crosstalk'* (crosstalk occurs when signals in a wire cause signals to be generated, via electromagnetic induction, in a neighbouring wire, thus allowing the original signal to be interpreted);

— *the detection of radiated emissions*, enabling information to be interpreted at considerable distances, particularly that emanating from peripherals employing high voltage and handling streams of information pulses.

Conversely, radiations from other sources can adversely

affect the performance of data processing equipment. Magnets brought close to magnetic media can erase recorded information, and such phenomena as radio transmissions, radar signals and the output from portable transceivers can disrupt computers and communications equipment.

The points mentioned in this section are far from exhaustive. The aim is to provide an insight, albeit brief and superficial, into the sorts of topics that are involved in the physical security of computer installations.

HARDWARE ASPECTS

Particular security features have been developed to protect computer equipment; for example, central processing units (CPUs), hard disks, etc.

A common facility is 'main memory WRITE protection', intended for large machines capable of multiprogramming. Where programs share the main memory, WRITE protection can prevent the program being executed from overwriting any memory location outside its own domain. Instructions to alter the bounds of the domain are available to the executive but not to the user program (otherwise the user program could redefine the domain to circumvent protection). It is necessary for control to be switched to the executive when required.

Other methods of hardware protection include:

- *privileged instructions*, ie those that can only be used by the executive;

- *parity provisions*, ie the use of an extra bit (for each word or byte) to facilitate checking;

- *watchdog timer*, running independently of the computer and able to signal abnormal (malfunctioning) computer operations;

- *hardware 'trapdoors'*, special switches and adjustable controls that may only be known to service engineers;

- *hardware checks for slow peripherals* (such as line printers);

- *main memory READ protection,* similar to WRITE protection but enabling a domain to be protected against the effects of READ instructions in the user program;

- *segment zeroing,* able to erase program and data residues from main memory (so preventing another program from reading the information);

- *READ-ONLY swap storage,* designed to protect against corruption of the overlaying parts of the executive;

- *stand-by facilities,* which may involve the provision of duplicate equipment able to take over operations in the event of systems failure.

Many of these facilities can be exploited to enhance the power of hardware to check itself. This is essential if modern complex systems are to offer useful self-diagnostic facilities (the declining cost of hardware has meant that it is increasingly cost-effective to design extra equipment for effective auto-checking).

Modern hardware is very reliable, and many built-in checking facilities are assumed. For example, disks and tape transports typically include checks to discern particular types of data error. Parity checks are particularly useful in this context. Many such provisions are included by the manufacturer as part of the equipment design, and the user may have little discretion. In other areas, however, he can organise his own checks as necessary.

SOFTWARE ASPECTS

As with hardware, there are various ways in which software can be designed to enhance system security. For example, application programs typically include controls to ensure that the correct processing is done on the correct files: checks are carried out to ensure that the right number of records are handled, that particular types of accidents have not occurred, etc. Similarly the operating system should include various features to provide a level of automatic protection. Such features may be part of the original design of the operating system or may be added at a later stage by means of a security package. Where security features are part of the initial design, they are harder to evade than if they are added later. The in-built security features of a package need be known only to the internal audit staff.

In general the software system is required to:

— identify each and every system user;

— maintain access controls over data, programs, processes and resources, so that only authorised users are allowed to access them in permitted ways;

— maintain a log of all usage for subsequent analysis by audit personnel, and alert appropriate staff in case of any attempted breach of the security rules.

The provision of software security, like other forms of security, necessarily involves trade-offs between costs of security and costs likely to occur when security is not provided. This again suggests that *perfect* security is an unrealistic goal, that the level of security should be appropriate to the circumstances.

Techniques for providing software security have been researched for many years. In the 1970s, for instance, the 'kernel' approach was developed involving the implementation of a concept that enforces formal security rules in a computer system (this is an approach that can be adopted for both hardware and software). The aim is to control access of active system elements like users, programs and processes to objects like information, registers, programs and terminals.

Here the kernel is expected to be:

— complete, in that it must be involved on every attempt to access objects;

— isolated in that it cannot be changed or evaded;

— verified, in that it must operate correctly in all circumstances.

There are some disadvantages in the kernel approach. It may cause a degree of inflexibility because the security rules cannot be separated from the mechanism that enforces them (though rule stability is an important aid to security); and bottlenecks may arise since the kernel mechanism must be involved with every access to objects in the system.

Where a system is initially designed to be secure, it should:

— enforce multi-level security properties that are mathematically provable;

— be realistic and have an efficient implementation;

— not be constrained by existing hardware;

— provide a flexible system base that can be extended to fit a variety of user needs.

Again it is worth emphasising that the significant costs involved in developing effective security provisions can only be justified if greater costs are likely with unprotected systems.

Typical software-protection provisions include:

— the elimination of software 'trap-doors' (which may allow access to forbidden areas and functions);

— automatic auditing, where a computer activity record is kept;

— a facility for reprisals by the system when an attempted security violation is detected;

— the protection of residue, ie stored programs and data after the user has finished with them;

— the protection of security parameters such as a record of authorised users and authorised terminals;

— the protection of memory and files;

— the verification of software (for example, using redundancy checks);

— the provision of comprehensive test programs;

— facilities to protect against self-corruption.

Any approaches to software protection should be considered in conjunction with other security provisions; for example, those related to hardware and to physical access.

CONTINGENCY PLANNING

The contingency planning requirement is largely self-evident: it is obviously desirable to be able to continue computer operations, using stand-by or other provisions, in the event of system collapse brought about by accident or deliberate intent. It is also necessary to achieve a rapid recovery so that normal working is achieved as quickly as possible. This dual contingency requirement can bring problems, mostly financial: can you afford to organise effective recovery measures when you are funding expensive stand-by provisions?

In devising a contingency plan various aspects should be considered. These include:

- adapting the provisions to the specific character of the operation (a stand-by computer facility clearly does not need to be more powerful than the current installation hardware);

- adapting the provisions, where necessary, to the external environment (if the site is prone to flooding or earthquakes the contingency plan should recognise it);

- the responsibility for implementing the contingency plan (there is usually a senior management, rather than a DP management, responsibility);

- maintaining documentation away from your site (and this includes documentation about how to implement the contingency plan);

- maintaining key files, crucial data, etc in a duplicated form off-site.

- allowing enough flexibility in the back-up provisions to accommodate unexpected circumstances (eg Was the original installation about to expand? Are key staff able to travel to the new site until recovery is achieved? Are the back-up provisions themselves subject to particular hazards, and is the stand-by site itself secure in these conditions?).

Stand-by plans should encompass all the relevant aspects; for example, hardware (on-site arrangements, reciprocal agreements, etc), software (duplication, priorities, supplier deals, etc), files and data (file re-creation, definition of vital records, etc), environment (flooding, high winds, subsidence, etc), services (water, power, air conditioning, etc), and personnel (absence, sabotage, etc). The plans should be flexible enough to accommodate the particular level of disruption: stand-by provisions in the event of system break-down will clearly be less extensive than those needed when the site suffers a massive disaster. The plans should emphasise that as much equipment, information, etc as possible should be salvaged, as a cost-effective practice.

Many companies offer stand-by facilities, recovery services and other contingency provisions. Sometimes, however, organisations prefer to set up their own contingency arrangements. In late-1988, for example, the insurance company Royal UK, based in Liverpool, set up its own disaster recovery centre after searching, without success, for a third-party firm that would provide cost-effective back-up. Peter Steward, Royal's computer centre manager suggested that the various firms surveyed were 'very expensive and are not able to provide us with the full service we needed' (quoted in *Computing*, 1 December 1988). A main problem was the lack of capacity ('The CPUs and disks were not large enough'). The result was that Royal spent £3 million on moving its Amdahl 5890 150 miles away to Northampton.

INSURANCE

Insurance, as a means of transferring risk, is a common means of offering protection. Any insurance cover intended to offer protection of computer-based facilities should be considered in the context of the company's overall insurance: overlap should be avoided but there may be particular requirements for computer cover.

Any insurance cover is generally expected to relate to three broad categories of loss:

- material damage;

- business interruption;

- risks to and from personnel.

Insurance can be obtained to cover system breakdown which can supplement the benefits obtainable under maintenance contracts. Indemnity, for example, can offer direct financial compensation, though the insured company will be penalised if the level of cover is deemed to be inadequate for the claim. The inclusion of an excess clause, to prevent many small claims, is commonplace. Other matters, beyond the scope of this book, relate to time exclusion, the use of a franchise, the condition of averages, all risks, selected perils, lease or rent provisions, secondhand computer cover, indemnity period, subrogation rights, warranties, etc.

FAULT TOLERANCE

It is worth mentioning fault tolerance as a means of emphasising that risks can be minimised by careful forethought: what is true for the design of individual computer systems is true, *mutatis mutandis*, for the organisation of the installation as a whole.

With our increased dependence on automated systems there is a growing requirement for continuous reliable operation approaching 24 hours per day, 7 days per week, 52 weeks per year. Thus Harrison and Schmitt (1987) point out that 'industries such as finance, transportation, securities and telecommunications have continuous availability requirements that can approach downtimes of not more than three minutes per year'. They describe, for instance, how a system can have operation in nonstop mode using various duplex hardware components:

- main memory;

- CPU complex;

- input/output controllers;

- system bus;

- power supplies.

It is suggested that this System/88 architecture, a design of Stratus Computer Inc, combines the duplexed hardware with distributed operating system software to provide a 'high-availability, fault-tolerant computing system'. Similarly, Charlton (1988) describes the significance of fault tolerance for operations jobs. (We may expect 'fault-tolerant' to acquire the sort of PR kudos once associated with 'user friendly'!)

The main point is a general one. Forethought can not only result in systems that are unlikely to fail but also establish provisions and mechanisms that will enable computers to continue working effectively should faults occur. Built-in fault-tolerance – at every installation level – represents a particular form of 'insurance' in circumstances where human life increasingly depends upon reliable computer operations.

AUTOMATED SECURITY

We have already seen that automated security, at various levels, can be designed into hardware and software (and into other installation features). This type of provision will be increasingly common in computer installations. One recent example concerns an IBM security system installed by Mastiff to protect the £3.6 million Kelvin computing project at Glasgow University (reported in *Security Gazette*, December 1988). Here hands-free radio tokens provide access control at interior doorways, and electronic memory keys provide lock control at the main entrance. All the system elements are integrated under centralised computer control, and access and egress are comprehensively monitored.

The mode of access control allows the researchers to work without the usual encumbrance of detailed security procedures. All the required doors unlock and open automatically for authorised personnel, while other individuals are effectively excluded from the building. People loitering near a doorway are detected, whereupon the security procedures are automatically engaged.

Today it is even possible to enlist the aid of robots in the quest for security. Thus Everett and Gilbreath (1988) describe ROBART II, a battery powered autonomous robot being used by the Naval Ocean Systems Centre in San Diego as a testbed in research. The aim is to develop a multi-sensor mobile security robot. Some years ago it was reported (for example, in *Computerworld*, 13 February 1984) that the American company Denning Mobile Robotics intended to develop robots for use as prison guards; and by 1986 Denning was testing a robot that could move, see, hear and smell. It is clear that there are many dimensions to the question of automated security.

SUMMARY

This chapter has emphasised the multifaceted nature of computer security. A spectrum of threat has been described, and examples given of disasters that have involved computer installations. Some principles that should govern the approach to security are outlined, with focus also on the nature of risk management.

The various aspects of computer security are considered with attention to physical security, hardware, software, and contingency planning. ('People aspects' have been saved for Chapter 4.) Attention is also given to the questions of contingency planning and insurance as different means of provided protection. Emphasis is also given to the increasing prevalence of automated systems – duplicated hardware, in-built software mechanisms, robots, etc – in the provision of security.

As automated systems become increasingly ubiquitous in human society throughout the world, and as we allow such systems an enhanced discretion over our lives, effective security is ever more important. Much of the security question bears on the possibilities of environmental hazard, system breakdown, poor design – usually inadvertent disruptions. However, attention has also been given to the possibility of deliberate acts that may result in theft, system impairment and total collapse of the installation's working. We need to pay attention to the possibility of mischief and malice, increasingly threatening in an uncertain world.

4 Malice and Mischief

INTRODUCTION

Many of the threats to the reliable operation of computer systems are inadvertent (Chapter 3), the result of component failure, unseen computer bugs, and such 'acts of God' as hurricanes and lightning (the BIS *Disaster Casebook* includes about a dozen calamities due to lightning strikes). But computer bugs that occur through human incompetence are no more disruptive than computer bugs deliberately introduced to cause havoc; and 'acts of God' are no more impressive than 'acts of woman (or man)' intended to sabotage computer performance – in this context, human beings are as inventive as any mythical deity.

There are many ways in which people can contrive the collapse of computer systems, and many ways in which they can exploit such systems in an illegal or immoral fashion. The corollary is that there are many different types of motivation impelling individuals to behave in ways that are strenuously (but not always effectively) resisted by computer owners, computer managers, politicians, policemen and other pillars of propriety. And computer criminals and mischief makers are often one step ahead: they can, at their leisure, think of hi-tech ways to steal, embarrass and disrupt – whereupon the authorities et al are obliged to react speedily to plug the gap. It is often the case that, by the time system security is re-established, the dissidents have thought up new tricks, new ways of illicitly attracting revenue, stealing information or hampering day-to-day computer operations.

This chapter profiles various types of computer crime and *non*-criminal modes of disruption (viruses, infecting journalese as much as computer systems, are considered in Chapter 5). There can be threat from internal and external people, from mercenary employees and from external individuals (hackers and the like) keen to flex their technical muscles. There is also the possibility of industrial action – which may or may not be morally legitimate, which may or may not be an example of malice and mischief.

Today there are many reasons why it is important to protect computer operations: inadequate protection could mean that hospital patients die, planes crash and bombs explode (when not intended to by due process). Increasingly there is legal pressure encouraging the effective safeguarding of computer systems: the UK Data Protection Act (1984) declares that security measures should be 'programmed into the relevant equipment' and measures should be taken 'for ensuring the reliability of staff having access to the data'; and hackers are increasingly likely to face legal sanctions. Just as there is a growing interest in countering inadvertent or 'acts-of-God' threats to computer installations, so there is growing pressure to counter the various types of threats posed by deliberate human contrivance.

COMPUTER CRIME

There are various species of computer crime and further types of behaviour that may, though not criminal, may be regarded as illegitimate. *Fraud* can be perpetrated in a computer environment and can cover various types of activity.

In English law there is reference to 'company fraud', 'conspiracy to defraud', 'fraud of investments' and 'fraud at play (cheating)' – though there is no definition of fraud *per se*. A reasonable definition is given by Michael Comer in his book *Corporate Fraud*:

> 'Any behaviour by which one person intends to gain a dishonest advantage over another. A fraud may not be a crime.'

It may be emphasised that computer fraud, computer-related fraud and computer-assisted fraud are all frauds. They are frauds first and foremost, and the use or abuse of a computer may be regarded as a secondary matter. Clearly there was fraud before there were computers, but the advent of computer-based systems give a new significance to a traditional immoral or illegal act.

It is often declared that many of today's white-collar criminals need to be computer programmers. One writer (Brill, 1988) observes that 'Many of America's finer prisons teach programming to inmates as a job skill! It's rather like teaching arsonists new techniques in incendiary device construction.' He cites the case of a teller, in a Brooklyn bank, who ordered the computer to transfer money to him and to make a number of fast money transfers from account to account to cover the shortage. He was taking up to $20,000 out of the bank every day, a hobby that was only discovered when the New York State Attorney raided the teller's bookmaker and examined betting records.

The creation of false transactions is a common type of fraud; for example, fake accounts may be added to a payroll file, enabling the perpetrator to collect cheques directed to non-existent individuals. A typical ploy is 'salami', where very small amounts are stolen from a large number of accounts and collected in a target account. Brill (1988) identifies two types of salami swindle:

— in the case of a 'soft' salami the transactions are modified by slicing off fractions, rather than rounding;

— with a 'hard' salami small amounts are deducted from a large number of accounts.

It is also possible to devise special programs that can supervise undetected special transactions, carried out via special coding to prevent incriminating details appearing on transaction printouts or audit trails. If the criminal knows that the system is likely to detect an illegal transaction then he may still be able to contain the evidence; for example, by directing the warning to his own terminal, where the signal of misdemeanour can be safely ignored.

Fraud and other types of illicit activity are frequently detected, though it is generally supposed that most computer-linked crime goes undetected. Examples* of such wrongdoing are given (further examples are given under Hacking, below):

In the USA, the Milwaukee 414s (a group of Milwaukee teenagers) penetrated a number of computer systems via a US Packet Switchstream service.

Four 13-year-old students at the Dalton High School in New York were arrested for breaking into 21 computer installations in Canada over a telecommunication network. The systems they hacked into largely used DEC hardware, as did the Dalton High School. Some of the systems retained standard user ids and passwords, which the students knew because of their previous experience with DEC equipment.

A San Diego High School computer was accessed by the pupils who changed passwords so that their teachers could not gain access to the system. They altered examination grades and assessments and generally tampered with files.

Two accounts clerks defrauded a major British leisure industry company. One sent bogus invoices for vast quantities of food stuffs, and his collaborator prepared false 'goods received' dockets and the invoices were duly settled. Their system had been running successfully for four years before they were discovered.

A computer liaison officer with a unit trust management company was able to defraud his employers by making bogus entries using fictitious names. Over a four-year period he stole £115,000. This individual had worked his way up from a junior position and thus had a complete knowledge of the administration procedures. His job was to reconcile share registers and cash records.

A businessman created some 50 companies which did not trade. False claims were sent to HM Customs and Excise for

*The examples are taken from *Fraud and Abuse of IT Systems* (R Doswell and Geoff Simons, NCC Publications, 1986); and from *Introducing Computer Security* (M B Wood, NCC Publications, 1982)

VAT purposes. In total £128,000 was netted over 13 months. Over a period of time he became familiar with the way claims were settled and was able to take advantage of this.

A systems analyst at a tobacco manufacturers altered a computer program to print fictitious credit notes for cigarette coupons which were sent to an accommodation address. He then collected the credit notes and exchanged them for goods.

500 disk packs were stolen from a data processing centre in Holland by a shift manager. A ransom of £290,000 was demanded. Pick-up of the cash in London failed. The shift manager was working out his notice which had been served on him by his employer.

A 19-year-old girl convinced her boyfriend to steal copies of computer programs from his employer, a computer bureau. She then tried to sell them to the bureau's customers.

A DP employee stole a customer history file from his employer. He used the name and address mailing list for his own activities.

A media librarian working for an insurance company was dismissed on 30 days' notice. During that time she replaced most of the magnetic data tapes with scratch tapes.

A 'near perfect crime' ended with a computer expert being jailed for 15 months for obtaining £45,000 from the Commercial Bank of Kuwait by deception. After the verdict the bank declared its intention to take civil action to retrieve the money by making a claim against the fraudster's home.

In this last case the perpetrator arranged for a program to transfer money from accounts of wealthy people to his own accounts in Kuwait. The aim was for the transaction to be made while Thompson was airborne for England and then for the incriminating details to be erased from the computer's memory. The money was transferred and spent by the fraudster within two months. Most of the money had been spent on paying off a £27,000 mortgage and on home improvements.

This case was reported in July 1983. It involved a complex legal wrangle concerning the law, computers, jurisdiction and the meaning of theft. The perpetrator, Michael Thompson, took his case to the Court of Appeal and there all the facts of the case emerged.

The crime Thompson had been charged with was theft, having obtained property by deception. Computers had been fraudulently programmed abroad to credit foreign bank accounts. A request was made in England for transfer of the balances to English accounts. The question was whether or not the property was obtained in England.

Thompson appealed against conviction on the grounds that the Crown Court had no jurisdiction to hear and determine any or all of the counts since the obtaining of the property referred to was, in fact, an alleged obtaining of property which the appellant had already obtained in Kuwait and not within the jurisdiction; accordingly the trial judge had erred in law in rejecting a submission to that effect by the defence at the close of the prosecution case and he further erred in directing the jury that the court did have jurisdiction to determine the counts. The facts of the case are reported in the *Weekly Law Reports* (20 July 1984). The conviction was upheld.

A 25-year-old computer terminal operator in an insurance company managed to secure for herself payments of pensions under 30 different names, making herself a comfortable income. Her scheme was a simple one. When pensioners died it was her job to enter the details at her keyboard. She had discovered that she could enter change of address instructions instead, so she did this from time to time. By using an accomplice's address the flow of monthly cheques was thus augmented yet again. When the auditors wrote and asked for confirmation that the pensioner was still alive – as they do from time to time – they naturally received confirmation by return. She was eventually caught because the controls were better than she realised, though not really adequate to prevent the original abuse.

The case of Equity Funding Life Insurance Company in Los Angeles, California is a case that has been widely discussed. Officers and employees set up some 63,000 bogus insurance policies in three years, worth some $1600 million. They sold these bogus policies to other insurance companies in the reinsurance business. Given wide television coverage as 'The Billion Dollar Bubble', the fraud involved mass collusion, including a computer programmer. The programmer produced the suite of programs needed to create the bogus policies, pay commissions, create fake reports, maintain balances, and interface with the genuine business.

The case was significant by virtue of its size. The computer was incidental to the main fraud. It was needed simply to process the huge amount of false transactions and paperwork.

Another significant early case occurred at the Union Dime Savings Bank. A chief teller embezzled $1.5 million by transferring money from legitimate accounts to fraudulent ones, and then withdrawing the money. He was able to make accounts appear in balance by shuffling amounts between accounts with very large balances. A very high staff turnover in the department allowed him to explain inconsistencies as being clerical errors. The system was completely on-line. This did not make the theft easier, but it did make it faster.

In a case in Devon in 1978 a former bank manager was convicted of defrauding his employers of £737. His scheme depended on the bank's method of handling spoilt cheques. In the clearing system these are segregated and sent to the drawer's branch for attention. The manager spoiled cheques drawn on his own account to pay shops and tradesmen. The cheques were met by the bank, but were rejected by the central bureau and sent back for attention. The manager simply destroyed them so that his account was never debited. The bank had good controls, so he was eventually caught.

One of the largest hauls reported from one incident in the UK was in 1977 when the cargo system at Heathrow Airport was apparently reprogrammed to divert a consignment so that it bypassed customs examination. Some £2 million of cannabis from Uganda was thus imported illegally. This is an illustration of the fact that cash is not a necessary ingredient for a successful coup. Almost any kind of goods or services are saleable somewhere. You do not have to have access to financial systems.

The Penn Central Railroad had a computer-system to control the routeing of freight cars. It was discovered that 217 large box cars were missing, and investigation showed that the programs had been modified to route them to a small railroad system. Here they were discovered, freshly painted in the livery of the supposed new owners.

A UK packaging manufacturer ran into problems paying for imports of board and paper from his suppliers in Sweden. The exchange rate was fluctuating, and the computer payments system was in a mess. The firm took on a temporary accountant to sort out the problems. He was good, and soon things were happy once again. The accountant was given authority to draw relatively large cheques – business was booming, and trade was good. There were some questions at the annual audit, but he explained away duplicate cheques by losses in the post. After three years he had drawn £218,000, and cleared the cheques into local accounts opened in the same names as those of the suppliers in Sweden. He was caught because he attempted to overdraw one of the accounts as he was preparing his get-away. The company published full details of the case as a warning to others.

In 1977 a female salaries officer was jailed at Winchester Crown Court. She pleaded guilty to 13 fraud charges (and asked for 67 others to be taken into account). She had the option of paying doctors' expenses by hand-written cheque or through the automatic system at the Hampshire Area Health Authority computer. Her fiddle was to pay the doctors via the computer and to pay to her own account hand-written cheques for the same expenses. Over a period of 2 years she amassed £12,000 in this way to augment her £250 monthly salary.

In Italy, France and West Germany there have been terrorist attacks on computers. The Red Brigade in Italy destroyed communications processors at eleven major installations. Average loss was $500,000. They produced a document, *Resolutions of the Strategic Directorate*, that depicts increased use of computers as part of a plot to maximise social controls. It describes computers as instruments of the class struggle, and claims that it is important to attack, unravel and destroy these networks of control. In France, politically motivated attacks were mounted against computers, which were seen as a symbol of capitalist oppression. Organisations were attacked simply because they had a computer.

Stanley Rifkin pleaded guilty to charges of obtaining £5.1 million from an American Bank. Rifkin accidentally saw the daily codes used by the bank to authenticate fund transfer messages. On impulse he sent a transfer, and used the resulting funds to buy diamonds. He failed to hide the diamonds and was dumbfounded when arrested. He claimed that this was the first indication he had that his impulsive scheme had really worked. His actions were inept. He failed to plan for converting the stolen sum. The diamond market is suspicious when someone unknown arrives with large quantities. It is probable that Rifkin effected the fraudulent transfer just to see if it would work. It was an experiment, to see what would happen.

In Sacramento, California, three employees of the State Department of Justice were upset by what they regarded as a miserly pay rise. They deleted certain records of arrest in the criminal record files. There are lots of similar cases. Sometimes employees have deliberately sabotaged equipment.

The case of Pettigrew is important because the admissibility of automatically generated computer evidence was considered by the English courts. The case concerned a burglary in the North of England. Some money was stolen from a house. It consisted of £650 in new £5 notes that the victim had obtained from the local bank. The police arrested Mr Stuart Pettigrew, who had in his possession some notes that bore serial numbers that might have indicated that they came from the same batch of notes given to the victim. The prosecution tried to put in evidence a print-out from the Bank of England computer indicating that these notes were part of a batch passed to the bank and into the possession of the victim. At appeal it was argued that the print-out was not admissible because the information had been generated by machine action alone. Pettigrew was acquitted.

A more extreme case of computer-linked crime concerns the efforts of the American peace activist Susan Komisaruk to destroy a military computer (reported in, for example, *Computer Guardian*, 3 March 1988). Komisaruk, nicknamed Katya, heard about an IBM 3033 mainframe housed at the Vandenberg airbase in California (the machine was reputedly part of a first-strike missile system known as Navstar), and she decided that the computer should be destroyed.

She packed a bag of tools, hitched a lift to the airbase and headed for the computer complex. Then she entered the complex (which, in fact, had been out of commission for four years), broke into the building and made for the computer. She destroyed the machine, worth about a million dollars, using a crowbar, a hammer, an electric drill and a bolt cutter. Finally she emptied a fire extinguisher over the debris. The next morning Katya called a press conference to publicise the event. In due course she learned that the computer was no longer part of the Navstar system, that Navstar was no longer at the base, and that in any case the purpose of Navstar is only to guide ships and aircraft. Komisaruk was sentenced to five years in jail and fined $500,000.

Computer crime, in one form or another, is commonplace throughout the developed world (and in much of the underdeveloped world). It is hardly surprising that where there are fewer computers there is less computer-linked crime. One writer (Bologna, 1988) discussed, with Soviet criminal justice officials, the incidence of computer crime in the Soviet Union. The officials were aware of hacking and other problems in the West, and welcomed information about safeguards for their own systems. No instances of computer crime in the Soviet Union were cited (the officials 'welcomed further computerisation of their operations but wanted reassurance that these innovations would not cause serious security problems' – a reasonable enough requirement, even in the age of glasnost).

HACKING*

General

It is perhaps inevitable that the term 'hacker' should mean different things to different people. Sometimes it denotes nothing more than the compulsive computer programmer eager to spend all waking hours working with the machine, exploring this or that section of coding, organising this or that technological 'fix'. This type of activity, albeit an unhealthy regime, need not be illicit or illegal: employers may even applaud such selfless devotion.

In another sense, *hacking* is used to denote criminal activity, the skilled use of a computer to perpetrate illegal acts of one sort or another. It is this type of hacking that variously excites the computer-naive public and stimulates demands for new security provisions and fresh legislation. We should remember that the term 'hacking' can have various meanings: the phenomenon of hacking is always of psychological interest but it does not always fall within the province of law enforcement.

The compulsive programmer has been with us for about four decades, throughout the whole history of electronic computing, but it is only over the last ten years or so that the phenomenon has stimulated the widespread interest of psychologists, law-makers and other professional observers. In 1976 Joseph Weizenbaum, an MIT professor best known for writing the ELIZA language-manipulation program, drew our attention to a 'mental disorder that, while actually very old, appears to have been transformed by the computer into a new genus: the compulsion to program'. He cited the programmers in the computer centres of which he had personal knowledge, remarking on 'bright young men of disheveled appearance, often with sunken glowing eyes'. Working at a keyboard their attention is 'as riveted as a gambler's on the rolling dice', as they pore over printouts 'like possessed students of a cabalistic text'. These people, seemingly indifferent to personal appearance and normal preoccupation, 'exist

*This section is based in part on Chapter 3 of *Fraud and Abuse of IT Systems* (R Doswell & Geoff Simons, NCC Publications, 1986)

... only through and for the computers'. They are, suggests Weizenbaum, 'computer bums, compulsive programmers ... an international phenomenon'.

We are not surprised to find that Weizenbaum represents the condition as a psychopathology ('far less ambiguous than, say, the milder forms of schizophrenia or paranoia'). Prevented from exercising his skills, the compulsive programmer is likely to become withdrawn and apathetic, a circumstance that can affect social relationships and other values that people might be expected to deem important. ('People get hooked. They begin to behave in a way that resembles addiction. They refuse food, they refuse their girlfriends'). Nancy Welles, writing in *Datamation* (15 June 1984), draws attention to the hackers' compulsive use of computers ('there's something addictive in the power of the hardware or software'). It is this compulsion that can induce some hackers to see every computer system as a challenge, a configuration to be 'tested', 'broken' or 'cracked'. We have already seen that some hackers strive to access 'closed' computer systems, not for pecuniary gain but as an intellectual exercise, a stretching of their own programming prowess. Managers and others struggling to protect sensitive information, financial deposits and other valuable commodities are understandably hostile to such hacker initiatives.

The antisocial nature of the hacking phenomenon is increasingly discussed in the literature, though the ethical status of the hacker is confused (see Law and Ethics, below). Tom Tone, for example, points out (in *TeleLink*, June 1986) that the 1960s individuals 'who were to lay the foundation stones for today's generation of hackers' were 'school dropouts and job changers, who turned to computing as a way of outsmarting everyone except the other members of their social group'. Such people did not conform 'to the then rigid American stereotype'.

Some joined the Massachusetts Institute of Technology (perhaps Weizenbaum spotted them) and began the MAC (Multiple Access Computers) project, intended to develop the time-sharing concept. Encouraged to test the multi-user computers to the limit, insights were gained that would inform future hacking endeavours. Moreover the developing hacker ethos was being conditioned by various social (as well as technological changes). Thus Tone comments: 'Today's archetypal hackers are 14 to 18-year-old school children with access to highly sophisticated gear. They have little or no regard to a society that has seen parents out of work and an equally bleak future for themselves'.

The hacking phenomenon has been publicised in various ways in recent years. The film *War Games* brought to the attention of a wide audience a range of activities that were already familiar to computer buffs. In this film a schoolboy first uses his microcomputer and modem to break into the school's computerized records and change his examination grades. Later, more alarmingly, he keys into a military defence network, and runs a war-game simulation which the system interprets as a real international crisis. Many computer specialists have applauded the film as a realistic scenario.

It is interesting that the screenwriters Walter Parkes and Larry Lasker researched the US strategic nuclear weapons establishment for two years before working on *War Games*. Parkes has said: 'We didn't know that the movie would have an anti-nuclear script when we started out ... You want to believe that nuclear defence is in good hands; however, the more we looked into it, *the more we realised that nobody is in control*' (my italics).

A number of real events have underlined the plausibility of the *War Games* fantasy. In 1984 two teenage hackers managed to 'break in' to the secret ARPA computer network, the electronic data exchange of the Pentagon's Advanced Research Projects Agency. This event caused an electronic chase across the US continent to the Norwegian Telecommunications Agency, including a visit to NORAD, the North American Air Defence headquarters in a deep bunker in Omaha, Nebraska. This (true) tale is remarkably similar to the plot of *War Games*.

The real-life hackers were pursued by the computers of such organisations as Stanford Research International, the Rand

Corporation, the National Research Laboratory, two east-coast defence contractors, two scientific research firms and several universities. Eventually two Los Angeles teenagers Kevin Poulsen and Ron Austin, were apprehended in their homes by six armed law-enforced officers. The boys had managed to crack a massive secret network using two microcomputers (a VIC-20 and a TRS-80), neither costing more than £140.

The hacker phenomenon has also been publicised by the sort of cases already described and, more recently, by the Gold/Schifreen case (see below). Century Publications launched *The Hacker's Handbook* by Hugo Cornwall in 1985, and the revised book, *The New Hacker's Handbook* in 1986. These books may be recommended for computer auditors and security personnel. (In *The Hacker's Handbook*, hacking is described as a 'recreational sport'.) Hacking is also the subject of various computer games (virtual training packages for putative hackers) that are available for home microcomputers. One such package reached number 9 in the UK charts (end-1985) of computer games software.

It is clear that today hacking is a multifaceted phenomenon. It may be practised for reason of psychological compulsion, as a means to indulging intellectual vanity. Or it may occur as a deliberate attempt at fraud, a means of accumulating wealth or power. It is of growing concern to managers and others charged with the task of maintaining the security of computer-based systems.

More Examples

A number of examples of hacking have already been given in this chapter. It is worth quoting other examples that have been influential in encouraging legislation or that are simply interesting.

In January 1989 it was reported (eg by Shelton, 1989) that an 'extremely dangerous' computer hacker, Kevin Mitrick, had broken into Leeds University's VAX computer and other DEC sites, causing $4 million worth of damage. The perpetrator, from California, stood trial on charges of computer fraud.

The Assistant US attorney Leon Weidman was quoted: 'This isn't just a child's game. He's a dangerous man; if he doesn't like someone he changes his credit reference. He needs to be watched so he can't do more damage.' Mitrick was also known to have accessed police department files and banking systems, and to have interfered with his own criminal records and a judge's credit rating.

On 24 April 1986 a jury at Southwark Crown Court, South London, found two freelance computer journalists, Steve Gold and Rob Schifreen, guilty of hacking. The trial, reckoned to have cost about £1 million, was widely seen as making legal history. One suggestion was that the judgement rendered the world of communications a legal minefield.

The Southwark jury decided that the journalists had committed crimes when they penetrated the security of the British Telecom Prestel system on nine separate occasions between October 1984 and January 1985. The defendants were charged under the Forgery and Counterfeiting Act, 1981: it was suggested that they had used forgery to gain unauthorised access to computers. Several charges were brought (one of the charges against Schifreen was that he had illegally accessed the private Prestel mailbox of the Duke of Edinburgh, a detail that received massive publicity).

The events that led to the trial* began in a remarkable way. Schifreen, while reviewing a piece of commercial hardware, happened to key a series of 2s when requested to log on to Prestel. This was accepted by the system, as was his guess at 1234 as the password! A couple of lucky guesses had put Schifreen on the system as a Mr G Reynolds, a British Telecom employee with privileged access to the network. Later, in September 1984, Schifreen dialled a computer and found two IDs and passwords – belonging to the Prestel system manager and system editor.

Schifreen discussed his success with a friend Steve Gold in Sheffield by telephone, which was later tapped by British

*The eight days of the trial are described in *TeleLink*, June 1986. Sentences of £600 (Gold) and £700 (Schifreen) plus £1000 costs were quashed at the Appeal Court in July 1987.

Telecom. He also informed Prestel, and the two journalists agreed that the leak should be plugged. However, Schifreen could not resist writing anonymous articles for computer journals and providing information for television documentaries. British Telecom, by now infuriated, accompanied the police to arrest the two men in March 1985. The prospect of a gaol sentence loomed.

At the end of the trial, Judge Butler commented: 'Forgery is a very serious offence. It will usually lead to a sentence of imprisonment, but I accept the facts of this case are of an unusual nature. So I am going to take a lenient view. This does not mean, however, that the courts will take a similar view in the future'. The defendants were ordered to pay £150 on each of the (nine) charges and to pay £1000 costs. It was decided, in mid-1986, that the defendants would appeal.

In recent years there have been many reports of unauthorised access to computer systems, and sometimes the lapses in security have an international significance. For example, in 1987 the OECD working party on transborder data flow collected evidence of unauthorised access to computers in Canada by West Germans, Norwegians and Americans. In one instance a German perpetrator penetrated the security of a mainframe computer operated by a research facility in Vancouver, and proceeded to alter file passwords and privilege levels. Here it cost $20,000 to secure the system, but the criminal was never caught. Even assuming that he/she could have been apprehended, the extradition costs would have been prohibitive.

There was also evidence that a Norwegian hacker had penetrated a Vancouver computer system in May 1986, but the extent of damage was not revealed. The authorities in Norway were informed but the Canadian High Commission in London received no response. In another case a Canadian firm interfered with a computer in the US, following a dispute over franchise fees: the Canadian company tampered with the tapes stored at the US organisation, rendering them useless (reported in *Transnational Data and Communications Report*, February 1987).

Towards the end of 1987 it was reported that a group of West Germans had broken into the worldwide Space Physics Analysis Network (SPAN), a system run by NASA to connect research centres throughout the world. Other US institutes and similar British, French, Canadian, Japanese, Swiss and West German bodies were also victims. All these installations ran under the DEC VAS operating system, consequently a source of anxiety to DEC customers. The hackers managed to:

— implant 'Trojan horses', allowing access rights to unauthorised users;

— use the penetrated system for various illicit purposes;

— collect user passwords before they were encrypted by the system;

— alter security checks to disguise the penetration of the system.

It was subsequently realised that various VAS versions had similar security loopholes, to the point that the hackers were able to penetrate 135 computer centres. They modified the systems so that they could enter the computers whenever they wished. The hackers even found that their illicit modifications had been automatically enshrined in security back-up facilities. The West German journal *Datenschutz-Berater* reported that user files had been adversely affected by efforts to cope with unauthorised penetrations.

Digital Equipment Corporation subsequently issued a mandatory operating system patch (IMPAT.010) to provide system security. The response of users was unenthusiastic, and many observers concluded that the NASA computers were still open. One writer (Gliss, 1987) remarked that 'Uninstalled patches don't work'.

In 1988 a 23-year-old man hacked into some 200 computer systems in various countries (reported in *Information Security Monitor*, November 1988). Edward Austin Singh was cautioned for burglary at Surrey University by Scotland Yard's Serious Crimes Squad, and US Secret Service agents flew to England to interview him. Singh, having worked on communications systems for five years, has claimed that he can gain unauthorised access to almost any on-line system.

He used Surrey University computing facilities to gain access to the 200 networks worldwide, and then he logged into Janet (Joint Academic Network), a system that links educational establishments in the UK. And he also used international links to penetrate multiple systems in Europe and the US. Singh is reckoned to have penetrated computers at the UK Ministry of Defence, NASA and various US military networks, including Millnet, the successor to Pirpanet, used to link military, scientific and academic institutions. He declared: 'I do not know what all the fuss is about. I thought the matter would blow over in a couple of days, but it does not appear to be doing so' (reported in *Information Security Monitor*, December 1988).

It is obvious that the skilled hacker has a multifaceted significance for such topics as industrial espionage, corporate success and national security. We can easily appreciate the pressures for savage legal sanctions when hackers, often a great embarrassment to senior managers and politicians, are apprehended. However hackers are sometimes praised, seen as free-wheeling loners, preserving individualism in an increasingly regulated hi-tech world. Hackers have been deliberately employed to expose security loopholes. Moreover it is sometimes perceived that they can serve society in various ways. In an article entitled 'The Moral Cracker', Baird et al (1987) suggest various societal benefits provided by characteristic hacker activity. It is seen that they variously:

- *expose system weaknesses*, enabling security loopholes to be plugged;

- *expose Big Brother*, so serving as an effective deterrent to government and corporate excesses;

- *undermine the Big Lie*, helping to demonstrate that computers are for everyone;

- *avoid perpetrating major frauds*, being interesting mainly in the exercise of skills (we have already cited exceptions to this claim).

Baird et al declare that crackers are far from being the greatest threat to corporate information resources: 'In-house programmers and other employees possess inside information that crackers usually lack ... disgruntled employees are greater threats to security than crackers.' Above all, hackers represent a major source of embarrassment and inconvenience to officials, managers and politicians – which is why efforts to discourage hacking are often intense (see below).

Techniques*

In order to break into a system from outside the established network, the system must have either dial-in line connections or be connected to British Telecom's Packet SwitchStream (PSS).

Dial-in Line Connections

Some systems have dial-up line connections as a matter of course, perhaps because they have remote sites which only require occasional connections. Alternatively some staff may require dial-up access to the central computer from numerous locations outside the established network. For example, salesmen may want to access the computer from customers' premises.

Even installations which do not have dial-up lines as part of their standard system may well have dial-up available for the back-up of their leased lines. In the event of a leased line being put out of action, the dial-up line can then be used for short-term back-up.

There are a number of other reasons why a computer might have a dial-up telephone line. Frequently with large systems, the computer manufacturer's technical support staff can dial in and review diagnostic and breakdown records which the machine automatically accumulates, and may even initiate changes to systems software on the machine. Remote mainte-

*This section is based in part on Chapter 6 in *Audit and Control of Computer Networks* (IJ Douglas and P Jolson, NCC Publications, 1986)

nance is itself a security risk, and the auditor or security officer should be aware that it is taking place, and consider the implications, for example:

- how reassuring are the manufacturer's assurances of the probity of their staff?

- can disks with sensitive data be disconnected from the system during remote maintenance?

- after maintenance has been carried out, should the operating system be reloaded from back-up, in case any unauthorised amendments have been introduced?

- how effective are any software boundaries to the scope and type of access which the manufacturer's technical staff can carry out on the system?

Whether either dial back-up or remote maintenance is used, it is important that the lines accessing the computer are not left permanently switched through, but rather that a manual connection has to be made when connection to the central computer is required. The enquirer is usually required to establish voice contact with the network control section and often to give a verbal password. The network control section then phones back the enquirer or the remote site at a pre-established number, and only then are they switched into the computer. Then they have to go through computerised sign-on procedures.

However, there is often a business need to allow dial-in access to the computer in such volume that it is not possible to rely on physically switching through to the computer system.

Dial-back devices are becoming available to help control dial-in access to this type of system. Essentially, a dial-back device is situated at the computer installation. It receives input messages, often carries out password checking against tables of passwords held in the dial-back device and telephones back to a predetermined number, which is associated with the caller in a table held in the dial-back device, to confirm that the call originated from an authorised number.

Obviously dial-back devices can only be used when the user

is phoning from a predetermined number which has been pre-programmed into the system. If this is not the case (eg for travelling salesmen, managers from their hotel rooms etc) the organisation is dependent on software password controls. This is also the case for packet switchstream networks. The special problems of networks which use the packet switchstream service are described later.

Packet SwitchStream (PSS)

Packet SwitchStream is a specialised data transmission service. To use Packet SwitchStream, you require a network user identifier (NUI), which is the charging code PSS uses for billing. It is also necessary to know the network user address (NUA) of the site to which you wish to obtain access. Network user addresses are generally published in the directory of the packet switchstream service.

The potential hacker is therefore likely to telephone a local public Packet Assembly/Disassembly station to gain access to the PSS system, and then either present his, or fraudulently present another user's, Network User Identity. The hacker then inputs the Network User Address of the installation he wishes to access. The hacker then has to sign onto the target computer in the normal way, usually by presenting a valid user id and password.

An increasing number of computers are becoming available through the PSS service, and therefore are available for attempted hacking.

Discovering Dial-up Numbers

Before a hacker can access a computer system, he must have the dial-up telephone number of that system. These can be easier to obtain than may at first be thought. Sometimes the dial-up telephone number can be obtained by phoning the computer department on their published voice number and pretending to be a confused user, and effectively obtaining the dial-up number by bluff.

Some companies even publish their dial-up numbers fairly widely within the organisations and therefore risk hacking attempts from employees, ex-employees or their associates.

Another way of gaining access is by using a device called an autodialler. Essentially the hacker programs his microcomputer to instruct the autodialler to try a range of telephone numbers. If he wishes to access a specific computer, he can restrict his search to the number set in use at the telephone exchange local to that centre, on the assumption that the computer centre is likely to be connected to its local exchange. When a data line is dedicated, the system records the telephone number and tries the next number. *The Hackers Handbook* contains the flowchart of a program to do this. Once he has found a data line, the hacker then must discover the protocol in use, and then the password and user id.

Once a telephone number has become known to one hacker, this knowledge may spread quickly throughout the hacking community. Hackers are often members of both formal and informal clubs and societies, and frequently exchange telephone numbers and passwords. One way they communicate with each other is via electronic bulletin boards. The bulletin board is an electronic version of a club newsletter. It is essentially a microcomputer connected to a telephone by an auto-answer modem. Readers can access the bulletin board from their microcomputers and read any information on display or leave messages, etc. The cost of setting up a bulletin board is essentially the cost of obtaining a microcomputer and an auto-answer modem, which most computer hobbyists have anyway, and of renting a dial-in telephone line. Anyone dialing into a bulletin board incurs the telephone connection charge on their bill.

Once hackers discover sensitive information about an installation such as telephone numbers, user ids or passwords, etc, they may leave that information on a bulletin board for the benefit of the rest of their group, and to the disadvantage of the computer installation.

Discovering User Ids and Passwords

Assuming a hacker manages to obtain a computer screen display of the target computer on his terminal, he normally must input a valid user id and password to gain access to the system. It is often not particularly difficult to obtain a valid user id since they are generally not considered to be confidential information. This can be done:

- by trying standard user ids which may be available in the system, and will be published in the manufacturer's literature, describing the system;

- by scavenging the waste paper produced by the installation. User ids are usually printed on computer printout;

- by trial and error. The system will often accept an unlimited number of attempts to input the correct user id, without generating a warning or closing off the terminal.

Assuming a hacker manages to sign onto a screen with a correct user id, he must then enter a valid password for the system. Users should be trained to treat their password as highly confidential, and therefore passwords should not be readily obtainable in the same way as user ids. However once, by whatever means, one hacker becomes aware of a password, it may be published on a bulletin board and therefore accessible to other hackers. The probability of any specific installation's password being available on a bulletin board is low. However, any installation unfortunate enough to have this information published is likely to be the subject of a significant amount of hacking.

If it is not available on a bulletin board, the hacker could again try bluff, and telephone the computer department and pretend to be a user who has forgotten the sign-on password. In a well-administered system there should be proper procedures for dealing with this sort of call, but in some cases the 'user' will be granted a valid password.

Another, even more worrying method of penetrating a system is by making use of standard user ids and passwords. Most systems have standard user ids, such as the systems managers user id (often SYSMAN, ADMIN or SPECIAL), and the chief operators user id (OPS, OPERATIONS, etc), and user ids for engineers, systems programmers, etc. When the system is supplied to the installation it often has these standard user ids set up with an initial password, often PASSWORD or all Xs. All this information is usually described in the supplier's documentation provided with every system, and also sold independently by the supplier.

Anyone who knows the standard user ids has an immediate toehold into the system. Even worse, if the standard password had not been changed, the perpetrator could submit the standard password recorded in the manuals and access the system with the high authority level of one of the standard system user ids, rather than with an ordinary user id. These user ids normally have much greater authority than ordinary users. The system manager user id, for example, usually has high-level authority to access the system, and can in many systems bypass password controls, and delete the update files and other resources.

If the hacker is not lucky enough (from his viewpoint) to find a system with standard passwords his next procedure would be to try likely passwords such as common names, etc. One computer security expert has stated that if users are required to change their password every month, the most common password used by computer programmers is the name of that month's 'Sun' calendar girl!

One risk is of trial-and-error-type access attempts. An extreme version of that would be to write a program which generated all possible combinations of alpha and numeric characters until eventually the correct one was submitted to the system.

Several types of control can be implemented against trial-and-error-type access attempts. Firstly, if the password is fairly long, the length of time to try all combinations could be enormous. A password requiring eight letters or numbers, for example, would need 36 (the sum of 26 letter and 10 numbers) to the power of eight options. This is approximately 2,820,000,000,000. Even with the speed of modern computers, it could take many days to try this number of options.

However, if the size of the password were restricted to four numeric characters, there would only be 10,000 combinations, a relatively easy task to test by computer.

The second main type of security measure against trial-and-error attempts is to log off the terminal after a predetermined number of incorrect access attempts. It is also important in this case to take action to prevent the user simply dialling in again. Either the terminal should be logged off for some time while an investigation takes place, or the user id used to make the access attempt should be revoked.

Discouraging Hacking

The following summarises some procedures that should be put in place to make it difficult for unauthorised hacking to take place:

  i) The availability of dial-in lines should be minimised. If dial-up lines are available, where it is feasible they should be configured away from the system, and only switched through to the computer after voice contact has been made and the reason for the use of the line confirmed. The caller should then be telephoned by the system, as further confirmation that the call originates from a legitimate number.

   However, we must accept that there are some instances where the large number of dial-in lines (legitimately required by the system) precludes such controls.

 ii) Dial-in telephone numbers should be protected as far as possible, as should the Packet SwitchStream Network User Identifiers and Network User Addresses.

iii) The applicability of a dial-back device should be considered.

 iv) Standard Network user ids should be amended.

  v) The controls over passwords should be implemented. They should be:

   − long (6 to 8 alphanumeric characters preferred);

   − regularly changed;

– not related in any way to the user and therefore impossible to guess.

vi) Unauthorised access attempts must be monitored, and action taken. After two wrong attempts, the user should be disconnected from the system and the user id revoked.

There has been much time and effort spent in making hacking a crime. For example, California lawmakers were actively considering anti-hacker legislation in the early-1980s, and *Computerworld* (16 April 1984) noted that the New York Attorney-General expected 'the Empire State to become the 21st in the union to make hacking a crime when a bipartisan bill is passed later this legislative session'. In noting the bipartisan approach, it was emphasised that the computer 'has created a whole new area of crime'. This type of statement is open to debate but it is clear that the development of computer-based systems is forcing a reappraisal of many traditional legal categories and attitudes.

In the UK there have been recent demands by MPs and computer security experts for hacking to be made a criminal offence. For example, Harry Greenaway, Conservative MP for Ealing North, has declared that hacking is a matter 'of the utmost gravity and steps must be taken, without delay, to close this serious loophole in the law'. Without such legislation, he suggests, the secrets are at risk 'that keep the West a place of safety'. In a similar vein, Conservative MP Neville Trotter, commenting on the activities of Edward Austin Singh, discussed above, observed that 'This man could have blown the entire Nato defence system and endangered the world. Yet, incredibly, he has committed no crime whatsoever'.

In fact hackers have recently been taken to court. Jim Fox, for instance, was prosecuted in late-1988 for conspiracy to defraud the National Westminster Bank; and operator Nick Whiteley was charged with damaging £60,000-worth of computer systems at three UK universities. Robert Morris, in the US, was interviewed by police for allowing a computer virus to wreak havoc in 60,000 defence and university installations (see Chapter 5). And we have already encountered Kevin David Mitnick, in jail in late-1988 and early-1989 for allegedly defrauding DEC and MCI Communications Corporation, and for transporting proprietary software across state lines. His lawyer, Alan Rubin claimed that Mitnick was being used 'as a scapegoat for a lot of hacking'.

Hacking continues to be a serious security problem. Dennis (1988), for example, has emphasised that 'hackers are an everyday problem for the industry as staff now have to worry seriously about keeping passwords secret, modem numbers safe and their company's secrets secure'. It could of course be argued that such requirements are essential to security awareness, and that the hacker has provided a service in 'concentrating minds' to such a degree. And it does remain true that the greatest threats to computer systems are likely to be posed by internal staff – who necessarily have intimate knowledge of how the systems work and the information they contain.

THREATS FROM STAFF

Most of the threats from in-house staff are obvious, and examples have been given. Incompetent staff can pose a massive spectrum of threat; for example, in generating unreliable software (Chapter 2), but threats in this category are inadvertent. They still need to be guarded against but they are scarcely examples of malice and mischief.

Deliberate threats to computer systems, posed by company staff, can arise from many different types of motive. The following have served as excuses when people have been caught tampering with in-house computer systems:

"I felt I could get away with it and not be caught."

"I am fed up with my job."

"I wanted to get even with my employer."

"I did not consider the consequences of being caught."

"Everybody else is stealing, so why not me?"

"Stealing from a large organisation can do no harm."

"Beating the system was simply a challenge."

"I did it because my close friend was sacked."

"The company's controls were so lax that everyone was tempted."

"If my employers had taken an interest in me it wouldn't have happened."

"The company deserves to be robbed."

"I did what my boss does. He cheats through his expense account."

If such thoughts can represent motives, then opportunities are often easy to find. These obviously relate to the particular job and skills of the individual. A programmer may have opportunities denied to an operator; a shift worker may be subject to minimal supervision; a manager can use his authority to divert scrutiny or suspicion. The more skills that a person has, the higher the level of potential threat. An analyst, for example, may need to enlist the aid of a sympathetic programmer in order to perpetrate a fraud, and where there is a conspiracy the likelihood of exposure may be higher.

In planning an effective security strategy, managers should take the above considerations into account. It may be necessary, according to the assessment of risk and the scale of potential loss, to vet individuals carefully before they are appointed, to organise back-up provisions for the event of internal sabotage, and to consider the financial accounting approach in the light of possible theft. In any event, the risks will never be totally removed; and some may derive from external environment factors – such as new legislation or government policies – over which corporate managers have no control. In such circumstances it may be impossible to avoid, for example, industrial action that results in the disruption of computer systems.

INDUSTRIAL ACTION

It has long been perceived by trades unions that a disruption of computer systems is a most effective way of putting pressure on company managements. Increasingly computer staff are in the front line of any industrial action. They may well be the first to be called out during an industrial dispute, not least because they can have an impact out of all proportion to their numbers. It is not surprising that in such circumstances staff relations in the computer centres are seen by managers as particularly important – even though they may not always seem to act according to this perception.

In the event of a strike by computer staff, management may be able to give a down-graded service to customers, but a partial strike of this sort could be funded by the union for much longer than an all-out strike involving all the staff of the company. This means that the strike may last for a long time, customers would begin to lose faith in the company, and it may be difficult to pay wages and salaries to non-striking staff (if payroll details are held and calculated on the computer). It is of course difficult for non-computer staff to take over the work of computer staff: only people working full-time with computers can hope to cope with computer demands and computer systems evolution.

Computer staff are increasingly being recruited to trade unions, and management needs to consider the extent to which data processing staff are held to be a separate and exclusive body in relation to other staff:

– Are data processing staff's terms and conditions of employment negotiated as a separate group within the organisation?

– Are they considered as technical or clerical staff?

– Do they have separate trades unions negotiating with management on their behalf?

– Does management treat them with kid gloves, or do they take a strong line?

Are data processing staff likely to have their career expectations fulfilled outside the data processing function?

– Is there a clearly defined career progression through the

organisation, or will the data processing personnel have to accept limited career prospects, and be prepared to seek a lifetime's career within the operations environment?

Do data processing staff find their work fulfilling, or have ways of satisfying grievances, apart from collective action, been fully explored?

— Has consideration been given to (for example):

  — rotation of duties;

  — career development planning;

  — in-house training?

Unlike operations staff within the data processing function, systems analysts and programmers tend not to be called to industrial action in quite the same way. The reasons for this seem largely to be historical, or because the withdrawal of their labour would not be so immediately noticeable to their employers.

In recent years there have been many examples of industrial action that has involved computer systems. The following examples are taken from the BIS *Computer Disaster Casebook*:

In 1979 a Post Office strike was spearheaded by 535 computer staff. The selective closure of computer centres disrupted processing of bills, cargo handling and engineering stores, accounting, System X development work, etc. The LACES cargo system at Heathrow was affected.

In a 1979 dispute with the government, the Civil Service Union called out thirteen hundred computer staff at selected installations. Delays were caused in the collection of £500 million a week in VAT revenue, and in the repayment of £100 million a week to traders. There was also a serious impact on payment of industrial grants, Premium Bonds, subsidies to farmers, payments to industrial contractors, arms movements, coin distribution, court proceedings in Scotland, shipping movements, payments to pensioners and the disabled, etc.

In 1983 the Banking Insurance and Finance Union (BIFU) called out staff in a dispute with an insurance company. Fifty sacked staff were reinstated and new incentive payment were agreed.

In 1984 the National Association of Local Government Officers (NALGO) called out Housing Department staff in a dispute with a city council over working with new equipment. NALGO eventually agreed to accept the council's terms.

The Association of University Teachers (AUT) called a one-day strike in July 1984 in a dispute with a university computer centre about the employment of two academic staff on short-term contracts. Work was severely disrupted at the centre.

In 1984 the DHSS decided to reorganise the shift pattern for computer operators at the Newcastle installation. This led to a strike of members of the Civil and Public Services Association (CPSA), the involvement of the Advisory Conciliation and Arbitration Service (ACAS), and eventual acceptance of a revised offer.

At New Year 1985/86 staff at the UK clearing bank went on thirty-six hours strike at five computer centres in protest at inequalities in allowances when compared with payments at other banks. The bank increased the allowances to prevent a further strike.

In 1986 a one-day national strike was called by AUT at university computer centres to protest against alleged government underfunding of universities. There was little impact on research establishments and university departments.

In 1985 a proposal by the Treasury to withdraw an allowance awarded to 6000 programmers and analysts caused a walk-out at the VAT computer centre in Southend, Essex. Staff in other government departments voted to strike the next day. The Treasury withdrew the proposals soon after they were submitted to the unions.

A 1985 strike was staged by computer programmers,

members of the Society of Civil and Public Services (SCPS), at Inland Revenue offices in protest at management plans to employ privately contracted programmers at the Telford, PAYE computer centre. Inland Revenue commitments to limit the future hiring of consultants were agreed.

A regional health authority in Northern England suffered a protracted dispute (1984-86) when staff boycotted computer equipment. Two projects – the Patient Administration System (PAS) and the Integrated Personnel System (IPS) – were delayed for two years. NALGO had organised a ballot which resulted in the boycott.

In 1987 British Telecom was involved in a strike involving 110,000 members of the National Communication Union (NUC) over a disagreement about the conditions attached to a pay and productivity package. There was an impact on commercial users of BT services and on the general public. There were reports of saboteurs cutting communications cables and using superglue on door locks of telephone exchanges.

These examples show, without any assumption of blame attaching to trades unions or management, that industrial action can be a potent force affecting the reliability of computer systems. Again we can emphasise that this is a grave matter with potential consequences for human health and human safety. Where human beings are key components in functional loops, there is always the possibility that the withdrawal of labour will cause total disruption of system operations. It is easy to see why this possibility should give managements an incentive to 'close the loops' (see Chapter 1): where human beings are excluded from day-to-day computer operations, there is clearly less opportunity for malice and mischief.

SUMMARY

This chapter has profiled the various types of threats posed to computer systems by deliberate human action. Attention is given to fraud, hacking, sabotage and industrial action. It can be seen that not all illicit activity involves *damage* to computer installations: indeed a 'salami fraudster' has a vested interest in the continued reliable working of the computer system. However, it is also true that fraud, of whatever type, represents damage to the organisation using the computer systems and also, in many cases, to the broader community.

Examples are given of fraud, hacking and other illicit activities. It is clear that there can be many motives for people intent on penetrating computer security. There may simply be the prospect of pecuniary gain, or the system may represent a technical challenge, a formidable test of personal skills. And we have also seen that political commitment or a sense of grievance can impel people to disrupt normal computer operations. All such possibilities represent possible threats to computer systems, and must all be considered by those people charged with the responsibility for developing security strategies.

5 Viruses, Worms et al

INTRODUCTION

In recent years increasing attention has been given to various interesting types of software designed to threaten computer security in characteristic ways. These items of software – viruses, Trojan horses, logic bombs, time bombs, etc – are able to achieve a wide variety of unwelcome effects in computer systems. They can, for example, cause stored information to be unexpectedly modified or completely destroyed; displayed data can suddenly start to behave in alarmingly unpredictable ways; and operational systems can be sabotaged, perhaps in circumstances that threaten human life.

First it is worth giving brief explanations of the main types of perverse software (more detailed descriptions are given later in the chapter):

- **time bomb**: a piece of illicit software that is activated by the computer clock to initiate a fraud, a disruption or some other sort of perverse activity;

- **logic bomb**: software that is similar to a time bomb but activated by a combination of events rather than by the computer clock;

- **Trojan horse**: coding illicitly introduced into a seemingly innocent program and designed to have characteristic illicit effects (similar to the 'bombs' but not necessarily needing to be activated by the computer clock or by particular circumstances);

— **viruses**: coding illicitly introduced into computer systems and able to 'reproduce', so spreading from one part of a computer system to another or from one system to another; and able, according to the type of virus, to achieve many different types of effects.

Most of the present chapter is devoted to viruses, seen as a particularly important type of security penetration. By virtue of their reproductive capability they can have cumulative and potentially catastrophic effects. A logic bomb, hidden in a program, can have serious consequences, but they are likely to be largely predictable by the perpetrator. By contrast, the virus – through its ability to progressively 'infest' a complex system – may have consequences that far surpass the perpetrator's intentions. Some viruses are more or less benign, reproducing happily enough but representing little more than minor nuisance value; but other viruses may threaten company survival or the reliability of military systems.

It is convenient to regard viruses as having three characteristic features:

— their reproductive capability (how and when do they reproduce?);

— their infestation potential (what subsystems are they likely to infect? how widely, if unchecked, will they spread?);

— their intended effects (what are they designed to do? play tricks with displayed digits or wipe out top secret files?).

It is now obvious that computer viruses come in many shapes and sizes (see Specific Viruses, below), represent many different types of threat, and stimulate much (often wild and uninformed) conjecture. As with many other new phenomena in Information Technology, there is extensive coverage in both the general and technical press, before the situation settles down and a modified IT landscape emerges. Today (in 1989), where computer viruses are concerned, we are very much in the 'hype phase'.

We frequently encounter articles in journals, newspapers and elsewhere in which journalists, with promiscuous fascination, declare that computer viruses are everywhere, wreaking unimaginable havoc with files and records, threatening the very fabric of the developed world. The hi-tech viruses have been likened to every imaginable biological counterpart, from the common cold to influenza, from AIDS to the Black Death. The virus *metaphor* is suitably fertile, stimulating talk of 'epidemiology', 'antibodies', 'vaccines', etc (see below); and those people with computer-phobic dispositions are given fresh opportunities to broadcast their alarm.

An editorial in the journal *Data Communications* (December 1988) suggests that what we are seeing is 'a bona fide media event, one that quickly captured the interest of an already computer-phobic public'. It is argued that while viruses do pose problems, 'frenzied media coverage' does not help technological evolution to consumer acceptance of home personal computers, networking and database services.

This chapter considers computer viruses against the relevant background; exploring, in passing, the significance of the 'life metaphor' and the origins of the first virus. Particular viruses are cited and brief attention is given to protective measures and to the question of ethics. The scene is then set for a description (Chapter 6 and 7) of specific computer applications where inadequate systems – containing software bugs or lacking immunity to viruses – represent a hazard to human life.

BACKGROUND

Many accounts have appeared in the press of people's first encounters with computer viruses. Josephine Bacon, for example, who runs Translation Express Ltd (Kings Cross, London) describes a typical experience (*The Guardian*, 19 January 1989). In October 1988 she was working on a translation when a ball suddenly appeared on the computer screen and began bouncing from side to side. At times it would 'kick' a letter into the middle of the screen. Bacon telephoned the dealer who sold her the machine ("Oh," she laughed,

"You've got a virus"). The bouncing ball was eventually diagnosed – by Dr Alan Solomon at S&S Enterprises, Amersham – as the 'Italian' virus, created at the University of Turin.

This sort of example is increasingly common – for example, among microcomputer users. The virus phenomenon is particularly worrying because of the uncertainty that it generates: it is difficult to know whether a system is infected, whether a virus will spring into action at some moment in the future. Some organisations in the US have tackled the problem by avoiding public domain software and downloading of files from bulletin boards, an approach that is inevitably unhelpful to enterprise and technological developments. Another ploy is to urge stiff prison sentences for virus makers.

Part of the problem is that the average computer is not designed to detect viruses. If strange things begin to happen then the standard security checks may or may not signal the anomaly, but the computer will be far from able to generate a diagnosis. This means that a computer system containing a virus will probably run and run, allowing the infestation to spread: in such a way the computer is induced to co-operate in its own mutilation.

It is not always obvious what measures computer users should take to avoid viruses and to remove them when they are detected (see Protection From Viruses, below). There is an increasing awareness that even 'shrinked-wrapped' software is suspect: there are cases where systems have been infected during development with viruses that are then passed on to purchasers. The situation become even more complicated by the fact that commercial anti-virus software can itself contain viruses, a situation that raises a host of conceptual and practical difficulties.

The scale of the virus threat may be judged in part by the attention it is currently receiving: not all the interest and concern derives from mere hype. Some observers argue that there is a virus epidemic (see below), and that illicit behaviour is being given an immense boost by virtue of the virus option (one noted PC columnist, John Dvorak, has suggested that unscrupulous software vendors may include a virus in their software products to seek out and destroy competitive software!).

In late-1988 more than fifty security specialists gathered at an Invitational Symposium in New York City recently to consider the virus question (the meeting was sponsored by the Information Systems Security Association and Deloitte Haskins & Sells). One expert observed that viruses were 'just a passing fad', but has now had a change of heart. A wide range of views were expressed and a report is now available from Deloitte. At the same time there have been calls for controls on virus testing. Robert Campbell, President of Advanced Information Management Inc (Woodbridge, Virginia) has described the Arpanet virus (see below) as a 'horror story'. He emphasised that it was fortunate indeed 'that there was no apparent malicious intent' and that it was imperative that 'immediate as well as long-term solutions' be reached.

It was reported (for example, in *Information Security Monitor,* December 1988) that Michigan had become the first US state to consider anti-computer virus legislation. Senator Vernon Ehlers was quoted: 'Because this is a new type of crime, it is essential we address it directly with a law that deals with the unique nature of computers. Of the Arpanet virus he echoed the common view, already indicated, that the US Defence Department were lucky that the virus 'was relatively harmless'. Again it is worth emphasising that not all security experts regard computer viruses as heralds of global catastrophe. For example, Charles Wood, a US security specialist has declared that people are too ready to blame viruses for any DP installation problems that arise ('Out of 1400 complaints to the Software Service Bureau this year, in only 2 percent of the cases was an electronic virus the cause of the problem').

Another expert, Samford Sherizen, president of Data Security Systems Inc (Natick, Massachusetts), has stated that computer viruses have heralded the end of the user-friendly computer arena. Some recent articles convey the new atmosphere:

Computer viruses can infect entire organisations,
Angel L Rivera, *Government Computer News*, 29 April
1988, pp 37, 43

Federal officials puzzled by computer virus attacks,
Neil Munro and Richard A Dance, *Government Computer
News*, 29 April 1988, p 89

Spread of computer viruses worries users, John Voel-
cher, *IEEE Spectrum*, June 1988, p 1 ff

At the same time, as we have seen, there is also the view
that computer viruses are a less potent threat than is often
believed. For example, Paul Karon (writing in *PC Week*, 31
May 1988), acknowledges that viruses have been damaging
and destroying data, and reformatting hard disks (numerical
data in a spreadsheet may be surreptitiously altered); but the
article is headed **The hype behind computer viruses: their
bark may be worse than their "byte"**. Thus there is
confusion about the nature of the threat posed by viruses.
Knowledge about what they can do is increasingly widespread. It is largely the extent to which they have penetrated
security systems that invites discussion.

We may expect the dimensions of the virus problem to
become clearer in the years to come. Ways of ascertaining
that particular system anomalies are in fact caused by viruses
will be enhanced as the phenomena are increasingly under-
stood. Already it is easy to decide that a sudden bouncing ball
on a screen, or displayed letters that suddenly collapse in a
heap, have some connection with a virus; but the situation
may be less clear with unexpected (and erroneous) data or an
unaccountably empty file. We all know that there are plenty
of ways in which computer systems can go wrong; it is not
always a virus that causes the problems. Before looking at
viruses – their characteristics and real-world manifestations
– in more detail it is worth mentioning the 'life metaphor' and
profiling Trojan horses, already encountered, as effective
relations of today's computer viruses.

THE LIFE METAPHOR

It is interesting that today *biological metaphors* are often used to depict aspects of computer behaviour. This is an interesting phenomenon in its own right, but it cannot be developed here. We need only indicate the practice to show the proper limits of metaphorical usage, to counsel against giving metaphors a *literal* interpretation.

This matter cropped up in connection with artificial intelligence (AI). When processing power, encapsulated in integrated circuits, was first added to terminals and other pieces of computer equipment, it was said that the hardware was 'intelligent' (as opposed to 'dumb'). The word *intelligent* was almost always put in quotation marks, to signal that the terminal (or whatever) was not *really* intelligent. Over the years, as the processing power increased, the quotation marks were discarded: intelligent terminals were commonplace. The metaphor had become transmuted into a new literal reality.

For many years efforts have been made to compare computer phenomena with aspects of the biological world. AI is the obvious example but there are many others. A decade ago, Karl Scheibe and Margaret Irwin (in *Journal of Social Psychology*, Volume 108, Number 2, p 103) discuss how programmers can come to personalise computers, even to the point of using personal pronouns (*New Society*, 24 January 1980, considers the research under the heading 'Computers as people'). More recently, further attention has been given to the question of personification. Nilsen (1984), for example, identifies anthropomorphic language used by human beings in the context of computer usage (thus computers can 'babble', a 'post mortem' may be carried out to analyse a system fault, certain types of functional synchronisation are called 'handshaking', etc). I myself have explored whether appropriately configured computer systems may be regarded as exhibiting 'life characteristics', and so may be seen as truly *biological* systems.*

Many observers have protested at a too literal interpretation of computer viruses. Thus the correspondent John Washington comments (in *Computing*, 25 August 1988): 'The Black Death is coming, there's nothing you can do about it.

Are Computers Alive? (Geoff Simons, Harvester Press, 1983); *The Biology of Computer Life* (Geoff Simons, Harvester Press, 1985)

Substitute computer viruses, and that's Tom Foremski's article in a nutshell (*Computing*, 4 August) ... many users are under the mistaken impression that a machine can be 'infected' simply by reading a data file – about as likely as catching a disease by watching a television programme with pictures of bacteria.' This nicely shows how confusion of metaphor with reality can cause people to misinterpret a hazard faced by computer systems.

Nobody really believes that computer viruses are *really* viruses but the metaphor can be used to suggest various useful approaches (see Epidemiology, below). The problem is when 'metaphorical elaboration becomes plain bad thinking. That point is where the metaphors stop being suggestive and are taken literally' (Roszak, 1986).

TROJAN HORSES

There is some confusion about definitions of 'Trojan horses' and 'computer viruses'. We are sometimes told in the literature that a virus is a special case of a Trojan horse and sometimes that they are quite different types of entity. It depends what feature you focus on and what your priorities are. The important thing, for our purposes, is to understand the phenomena: semantic logic-chopping is a secondary concern.

It is generally recognised that Trojan horses began in the US in the late-1970s, at a time when electronic bulletin boards were becoming widespread. Programs could be downloaded from bulletin boards and uploaded to them, and it was not long before someone realised that it was possible to upload a program that would destroy all the data in the bulletin board. In this context, the idea developed that a Trojan horse was a program that, unsuspected, carried out some malicious or mischievous activity.

Typically a Trojan horse is contained in a legitimate program and causes an illegitimate action: it may, for example, obtain a password or modify records in protected files. The Trojan horse, as a functional 'parasite', may have no interest in destroying the host. It may render the system transparent to an illicit user, but the system may continue to function normally.

The concept of the 'worm' program, related to Trojan horses, was developed nearly a decade ago (Shoch and Hupp, 1982). It is characteristic of the worm program that it can 'relocate': it can, for example, copy itself to another machine on a network (worms are chronological ancestors to viruses but some modern writers equate the two). Worm programs can serve various purposes. They can help to sabotage systems, but can also perform useful tasks. Shoch and Hupp show that, for example, worms can be used as diagnostic tools for an Ethernet installation; and it is also suggested that they can be employed as billboards or alarm clocks.

There is also the idea of programs that can attack each other, developed in a game called Core War (Dewdney, 1984); and these, with Trojan horses and autorelocatable programs, prepared the way for computer viruses. Thus Davis and Gantenbein (1987) declare that a computer virus is a 'Trojan horse program with the capability to autorelocate and attack other programs' (see also What is a Virus?, below).

Today Trojan horses are still being illicity transferred into bulletin boards, sometimes erasing or scrambling the files of unsuspecting users. Some of these programs, conveyed via telephone links, began their activities as soon as they arrive; some can lurk in legitimate software for months, effective time bombs awaiting a trigger. An article in *The New York Times* (19 May 1987) describes five different types of Trojan horses.

WHAT IS A VIRUS?

Some of the main characteristics of a computer virus should now be obvious. It is, for example, a benign or malign program (within legitimate software) that is unsuspected by the user (until it functions) and that can reproduce itself throughout a system or a network. There are in fact many definitions, in the literature, of computer viruses.

Cohen (1987) defines a computer virus as a program that

can infect other programs by altering them to include a copy of itself (it is allowed that the virus may evolve during the reproduction process). It is recognised that a virus may be a special instance of a Trojan horse, distinguished by its talent for self-replication and for thus transporting itself from one area to another.

When a virus functions, it causes a copy (or copies) of itself to be injected into other programs and/or files, so progressively expanding its influence. In this way it can spread to many of the regions – user identities, virtual machines, memory spaces, etc – within the computer configuration or within the network of systems. We have seen that a virus can destroy data, cause a user to surrender his ID and passwork, and play tricks (the 'bouncing ball').

One writer (Fak, 1988) defines a virus as 'any code that would copy itself to programs which the code had written access to when it was run'. Here it is suggested that a virus may or may not contain a logic bomb, but that it is inevitably a Trojan horse, 'existing without the knowledge of those who run the program, Cohen (1987) emphasises that every program that gets infected 'may also act as a virus and thus the infection grows', though the infestation may be generally 'nondestructive' (Burnham, 1985 – though times have changed in the last few years). Goodwins (1988) sees viruses as always unwelcome, whether they are nominally benign or malicious. In fact viruses have already achieved dramatic effects: a virus in Prestel destroyed masses of data; a doctor lost all his patient records; a satellite net was closed for eighteen months. Part of the problem is that a virus may take steps to avoid detection, until it is too late.

Some of the key characteristics of viruses can be summarised:

- a virus can copy itself, or a mutated version of itself, into another file or disk. Typically, if a disk carrying a virus is put into a computer, the virus is loaded into the machine and copies itself onto every other disk that is used. The virus can also copy itself down telephone lines or via network connections. If a person is looking for a virus, he

may not recognise it if it has been copied in even a
slightly mutated form;

- a virus, as an effective parasite, has a degree of
autonomy: it can run without being explicitly called by
the user of the computer, a trick it may manage by
altering the operating system;

- viruses can have all sorts of different effects, from
writing an amusing slogan on a screen to causing a
complex system to crash. As with hacking, the motives of
the perpetrators are many and varied. Mere fun may be
the motive, or there may be an attempt to disrupt a
computer network for military reasons;

- a virus may take steps to avoid detection, as with the
deliberate evolution of different species of virus (which
may have very different effects to those of the parent
species). It is also of interest that some virus-detection
programs do themselves become infected, and so are then
only capable of degraded performance (see Protection
From Viruses, below).

The main features of the computer virus are generally
agreed, but there is still considerable debate about the extent
of the infestation. Do viruses represent a widespread problem? Do they have only limited local nuisance value? Or is
there a global threat, an escalating hazard of epidemic
proportions?

AN EPIDEMIC?

Much of the commentary – in both the general and technical
press – on viruses suggests that the problem is a veritable
epidemic. Thus an article by Tom Foremski (*Computing*, 4
August 1988) is headed 'Beware an invisible epidemic'. And
according to Josephine Bacon who runs Translation Express
Ltd (in London), the virus expert Dr Alan Solomon has
commented* that the problem of destructive software 'is

*In a helpful comment to the National Computing Centre (23rd January 1989) Dr
Solomon denied that he had said anything about 'epidemic proportions' but declared
that the problem was certainly getting worse.

growing to epidemic proportions' (reported in *The Guardian*, 19 January 1989). Paradoxically, Solomon, who addressed a BCS branch in November 1988, was also quoted as saying that viruses 'are very rare indeed. I'm getting about one or two reports a week which turn out to be genuine viruses' (*Computing*, 24 November 1988).

One expert (Gibson, 1988), in the last of a series of four articles, talks about 39 different strains of software viruses that have been identified. Elsewhere (*Computers and Security*, Volume 7, Number 4, 1988), statistics from various sources are cited:

- there have been 250,000 virus outbreaks (in the States);

- some 50,000 floppy disks were infected at one university;

- about 10,000 virus attacks have hit stand-alone PCs;

- somewhat under 10% of the Fortune 500 firms have been victims of viral infections of their information systems.

It is emphasised that many statistics are inflated (a symptom of the hype phase). A trade organisation told *Computers and Security* that one of its members had received 'almost 10,000 computer viruses from individuals and companies that were attacked' – a virus expert subsequently found that only 4%–5% were actual viruses. But even a figure of 400–500 viruses active in the US seems excessive (see Specific Viruses, below).

We need to distinguish between actual viruses (often identified by names) and the extent of the infestation. It has been reported, for example, that a number of viruses have plagued the Apple Macintosh community, with computers at NASA and at Apple's US headquarters affected. One virus, dubbed Scores, is said to have infected more than 200 Macintosh computers at NASA's Washington offices. Before indicating some well-known (and not so well-known) computer viruses, it is worth mentioning what is generally thought to be the first example of such an entity.

THE FIRST VIRUS

The first computer virus was designed and tested by Fred

Cohen in 1983 (Dembart, 1984): on 3rd November the virus was conceived of as an experiment to be presented at a weekly seminar on system security (see the accounts in Cohen, 1985; and Cohen, 1987). (The terms 'virus' was suggested by Len Adleman.) After eight hours of work on a VAX 11/750 system the first virus was ready for demonstration. Permission was granted to perform experiments, and it was on 10th November 1983 that the virus was first demonstrated to the seminar. In five trials the time needed to crash the computer averaged less than thirty minutes. Cohen was so successful that the administrators refused to let him continue the experiments because of their concerns about security. When it was reported that use of the virus would quickly grant an attacker all system rights, further tests were banned.

The virus concept was first made public in 1984 at the National Computer Security Conference when Fred Cohen published his results. It was established that a computer virus could infect some systems in only a few minutes. A massive new security issue was soon apparent. In Europe, Rudiger Dierstein presented a paper, 'Computer Viruses: A Secret Threat', to the 1986 Securicom meeting in Paris; and he emphasised the statement '*You may trust any program – and hence any computer systems – just as much or as little as you trust the programmer who implemented it*'.

SPECIFIC VIRUSES

Many different types of viruses have been designed and detected; and they are variously nameless or assigned a number or word (often they are named after their inventor). The viruses vary in their effects, as do biological viruses in the real world. The specimens mentioned in this section are examples only: the list is far from exhaustive.

In late-1988, students at Southern California universities were warned of a quickly spreading West German virus that was disrupting the operation of Apple Macintosh computers. Chris Sales, computer centre consultant at California State University (Northridge) declared: 'This thing is spreading like mad. It originated in West Germany, found its way into the UCLA network and in a short time infected us here.'

Students and disks were being screened before they were allowed access to the computers (reported in *Information Security Monitor*, December 1988, p 8).

Geoffrey Taylor, writing in *The Guardian* (13 July 1987), describes a virus that interfered with the operation of his Tandy computer: unwanted characters had inserted themselves in various places in written text ('Although the virus shows a preference for numerals it will attack letters when no numerals are present').

In *Computing* (5 January 1989) it was suggested that IBM may have given a virus to clients. About one hundred customers attended a course at IBM's European education centre at La Hulpe outside Brussels. IBM subsequently sent them all a letter warning that they may have contracted a virus from one of the personal computers at the centre. The customers were advised to quarantine any machines or disks that may have had contact with the virus ('Any infected customers can get in touch with us to isolate and eradicate the contamination').

New strains of viruses were detected in late-1988, some of which affect IBM compatible personal computers. One virus is in encrypted form; another is intended to delete program files. The '1813' virus infects the file rather than the boot section, and then makes it expand by 1813 bytes. Alan Solomon has observed that 'Unfortunately, there's a bug in the virus that makes the files grow too long'. Another virus, the '648', generates 648 bytes of unwelcome growth.

A virus has also been detected in commercial software produced by the US Aldus Corporation, and it was found that an entire network at Aldus' Seattle headquarters had been infected. This virus, dubbed 'NVIR', was first found in the Freehand applications software.

Another specimen, the 'retro-virus' able to live inside popular shareware programs, has been detected in the US. It attaches passive carrier clones of itself to other executable files – on the chance that the infected files will encounter other systems that contain 'infectable' programs. The virus uses a hidden 'flag' to communicate with the infected clone carrier executables. The operation of the flag can mislead the user into thinking that the system is clean. But later, perhaps in a matter of months, the virus again makes its presence felt.

Some viruses, as we have seen, are presumably intended to be nothing more than amusing. We have already encountered the bouncing ball of the Italian virus. The IBM Christmas tree virus is also famous, as is the 'cookie monster' program that forces users to spell out the word 'cookie' before access to the files is allowed. More serious is the Lehigh virus that is designed to destroy the first fifty sectors of a disk.

An American-made computer sex game, 'Leisure-Suit Larry' (distributed in the UK by Activision of Reading), is intended to run on IBM PCs and PC compatibles. If, in the game, a man dates the wrong kind of girl he is likely to be told: 'You have contracted a nasty disease. Game over.' Unfortunately, pirate versions of the game are now known to contain a real (computer) virus infection that destroys all the programs and data files on the hard disk of the owner's computer. A spokesman for International Data Security has referred to 'distressed calls from businessmen'; and an Activision spokesman has recommended that pirated versions of Larry be avoided.

In late-1987 a virus attacked the US National Aeronautics and Space Administration's *Space Physics Analysis Network*, a semipublic bulletin board. It is reported (in *Computers and Security*, 7, 1988) that the Hamburg Chaos Computer Club (CCC) in West Germany bypassed the system's security and planted one or more viruses.

It is worth saying a little more about the Christmas tree virus, already mentioned. In December 1987 a student at the University of Clausthal-Zellerfeld in West Germany decided to put an electronic Christmas card into the university's computer system. A user had only to write the command 'enter: Christmas' and he would be confronted with a tree (plus a greeting) on the screen. In fact the university system was linked, via Braunschweig Technical University to the European Academic and Research Network (EARN), its American equivalent (BITNET) and the IBM VNet.

Before long the Christmas tree appeared at the Weizmann Institute in Israel, various universities (Bochum, Heidelberg, Stuttgart, Zurich, Bonn, etc) in Europe, and the University of Tokyo. Paul Setze, manager at the University of Illinois, commented (on 9th December): 'The Christmas program is reproducing itself faster than rabbits. We have eliminated over 300 of them which reached us from Ohio State University.' Then Clausthal, the source of the infection, found it was receiving Christmas-tree greetings from Missouri, the Netherlands and other places. The authorities managed to track down the culprit but were then uncertain what to do with him ('It is not as if he had spied on computer data or destroyed any programs. The trees have merely formed an avalanche which has overloaded the system … we have to do something to deter other people').

The Amiga virus, reported in November 1987, was recognised as one of a number that threatened IBM PCs. One virus typically occupies the Command.Com file. When the operating system is loaded from an infected disk, and a command (eg 'copy' or 'dir') is typed, the infection spreads to any disk that has a Command.Com. After four replications the files are wiped clean, as has happened at Lehigh University in the US (hence the name of the virus).

Another virus, with a growing reputation, is the 'Brain' program (Highland, 1988). This virus is said to have been written by Amjad Alvi in Lahore, Pakistan, to protect his software. It has now spread to Britain, the US and elsewhere, 'far beyond the intentions or expectations of its author' (Lammer, 1988). 'Brain' infects system disks by occupying two sites, at the same time taking steps to disguise its presense. The virus appears to be largely benign (Lammer: 'It does not appear to be particularly malignant. …'), but has been harmful on occasions (Highland: 'The virus was at times destructive').

The 'Brain' virus* is said to be the first to strike in the US outside of a test laboratory (it was reported to the University

---

*Copies of 'Brain' have even been offered for sale (see the report in *Computers and Security*, December 1988, p 537)

of Delaware Computer Centre on 22nd October 1987). It is so called because it writes 'Brain' as the disk label on any floppy disk that it attacks; it is sometimes also called the 'Pakistani' virus.

We have already met the 'Scores' virus, now known to have infected more than 50 per cent of the 400 Macintosh computers at the NASA Washington offices. It is detected by altered symbols that appear in two files, Scrapbook and Note Pad. Users see, instead of the Macintosh logo, a symbol that resembles a torn piece of paper. A NASA spokesman has stated that the virus does not attack data (Charles Redmond: 'We have no record indicating anyone has lost anything important').

In late-1988 a virus devised by the student Robert T Morris jammed more than 6000 military computers across America. This virus, known as the 'Internet' virus, has revealed that Pentagon computer security is highly vulnerable to penetration. The event has provoked massive discussion in both the general and technical press (see, for example, Rosenberg 1988; *The Daily Telegraph*, 7 November 1988; Betts 1988; Anderson 1988; and Alexander 1988). The scale of this penetration is indicated by the bare facts of the case. The problem lasted for about 48 hours and thousands[†] of computers at up to 700 institutions were infected. There was a virtual shutdown of large research networks, including the Arpanet, the NASA network and the NSFnet. The article headings signal the gravity of what is taken to have been the most massive threat so far posed by a computer virus:

'Viral invader spreads havoc in American computers'

'Virus ravages thousands of systems'

'US virus sends chill down UK networks'

At the same time the 'relatively benign' nature of the virus suggested that it would be difficult to prosecute the perpetrator.

Some viruses are time bombs, capable of spreading to

[†]Alexander (1988) talks of estimates of up to 250,000 affected systems.

various systems and of being triggered after weeks or months. There has been much talk of Friday 13th viruses. In early-1988, for example, it was rumoured that an employee of the Hebrew University of Jerusalem left a viral time bomb in an IBM mainframe system. In fact on every Friday and the 13th of each month, the affected computers were caused to slow almost to a stop. The virus, when detected, had already been widely distributed.

In January 1989 – which contained a Friday 13th – there was fresh trepidation about lurking viruses. It was reported that the '1813' virus sprang into action in various places and firms were forced to take remedial action. Files were wiped and operators were panicked into destroying whole programs. '1813' is thought to be much the same sort of creature as the Jerusalem virus.

The bestiary of computer viruses continues to grow: we are witnessing a massively enlarging spectrum of 'biological' evolution. We have seen that many viruses are potentially very harmful, capable of surreptitious infiltration and of altering or destroying crucial files. Sometimes, a sense of humour seems to be the only inspiring motivation. The '1701' virus, for instance, does nothing more than cause all the letters displayed to slowly slide down the screen and disappear; other viruses cause the letters to fall into a heap at the bottom of the display. Whether computer viruses represent mere nuisance or the threat of social catastrophe, computer users – unless they are virus makers – have an interest in their prevention and removal.

EPIDEMIOLOGY

We have already seen that many efforts have been made to regard biology phenomena as nice metaphors for what can happen in computer systems (see The Life Metaphor, above). It is worth developing this theme to indicate how far the 'virus disease' metaphor, in particular, can be expanded to offer fruitful approaches to the prevention and cure of computer viruses.

An attempt has been made, for example, to depict the

human immune system as an information systems security reference model (Wood, 1987). Here analogies are seen between various biological immune provisions and the mechanisms that can be designed to enhance computer security. For instance, antibody programs are envisaged that could counter specific types of attacks on a computer system, with such programs automatically generated by the host system or ported from another facility. Such artificial antibodies could be built to counter a particular type of threat (such as guessing passwords or brute-force searching for security parameters).

In this imaginative way, Wood discusses other immunological provisions and their computer analogues; for example:

- white blood cells: travelling programs that check system internals;
- antigens: pattern recognition techniques applied to system logs;
- free radicals: errors and omissions neutralisers;
- inflammation and fever: continuous processing with problem isolation;
- acquired immuno-deficiency syndrome (AIDS): attacks initiated by internal controls.

It can be argued that this is a singularly fruitful approach in the age of the computer virus. Murray (1988) in fact specifically applies an epidemiological model to the analysis of computer viruses. Having discussed the suggestive character of the word 'virus' (and the Greek origins of the word 'epidemic' – literally, 'upon the population'), he expands the metaphor in interesting ways.

In particular it is proposed that many of the traditional epidemiological categories are useful in approaching the prevention and cure of computer viruses. Thus Murray observes:

'Community, population, carrier, portal of entry, vector, symptom, modes of transmission, extra-host survival, immunity, susceptibility, sub-clinical indicator, effective transfer rate, quarantine, isolation, infection, medium and culture are all terms from epidemiology that are useful in understanding and fighting computer viruses.'

These various terms and concepts are applied in the computer systems environment to suggest an approach to system security. For example, a virus may be expelled (sneeze, SENDFILE) on a vector (mucous, data object, file or program). Similarly, computer analogues can be found for typical biological defences (hygiene, prophylaxis, antidotes, purges, etc), and it is useful to explore such concepts as natural immunity, the effect of the incubation period and the identification of the pathogen.

Again it is worth emphasising that metaphor can offer a useful insight into seemingly intractable problems. This is true in the domain of computer viruses as it is true in other areas where analogies can be perceived between artificial systems and their biological counterparts. The task with computer security, as elsewhere, is first to understand the problem and then to consider ways of tackling it. The epidemiological model, linked as it is to an awareness of biological phenomena, is potentially fruitful in this regard. It is conceptually useful, but it is important to appreciate that other strategies also can be developed to enhance the security of computer systems.

PROTECTION FROM VIRUSES

General

As with computer security in general, there are many ways of tackling the virus problem in particular. Systems can be designed to detect, where possible, a virus infestation. Software products can be acquired to offer an anti-virus service (see below). A virus expert can be called in the remove detected viruses. Staff can be screened, where practical, to exclude those with an inclination to code viruses into software during the various phases of system development. And legal penalties for virus makers can be introduced to provide effective sanctions.

Recommendations for combatting computer viruses have been made by many individuals and groups. For example, Keefe (1988) describes a small working group (of network manufacturers) that has produced a set of recommendations. (As with all security measures, a balance must be struck between the costs of the solution and the costs likely to be incurred by an unprotected system.) The group suggests, for example, that

- all software should be acquired from reputable sources;
- only shrink-wrapped or securely-contained software should be purchased;
- back-up software should be produced as soon as the purchased software is unwrapped, and stored off-site;
- all software should be reveiwed, before installation, by a systems manager;
- new software should be quarantined on an isolated computer;
- back-up software and data should be made at least once a month and stored for at least a year to counter time-bomb viruses;
- access to programs and data should be restricted;
- programs should be frequently checked for size changes, signs of virus infiltration;
- shareware and freeware programs, easy entry points for viruses, should be quarantined;
- contaminated software should be quickly removed when the infestation is detected.

It is obvious that the only sure way of avoiding contamination is to avoid anything that might carry a virus, and this may be easier said than done. It is obvious that programmers should be trustworthy and that security measures should bear on all components of the system, as appropriate. It may be helpful to enter all programs as source code, to allow inspection by independent persons; to compute a cryptographically sound checksum for each protected program and process; to isolate production and development runs from each other, etc.

There are various system design measures that can protect against computer viruses. Cohen (1987), for example, discusses the relevance of partition models, flow models, limited interpretation and precision problems. It may however be impossible to prevent viruses completely, for the same reason that it is impossible in the biological world: there is an impulse to *sharing* which is essential to the community of active agents (computers are developing, via networks, their own communities).

The question of curing a virus presupposes an effective strategy following detection. Cohen considers how the presence of a virus may be determined (some viruses will, nonetheless, be able to circumvent the detection mechanisms), discusses evolutionary aspects, and proposes how a limited viral protection could be achieved. He quickly dismisses the idea that viruses could be spontaneously generated: behind every computer virus there is a mischievous or malicious human being.

In the same spirit, Pozzo and Gray (1987) emphasise that 'executables' can only be protected from modification by a malicious virus in two general ways:

- by rendering the executable immutable;

- by detecting any changes to the executable prior to execution.

Ways of accomplishing these objectives are proposed. Particular stress is laid on the value of encryption in this context. Cryptography can be used 'to protect the integrity of executables and thus provide a mechanism to detect viral spread and limit potential viral damage'.

Various anti-virus proposals were made at the 10th National Computer Security Conference (reported in *Computers and Security*, 7, 1988). For example, Catherine Young of the Office of Research and Development of NCSC presented a paper,

'Taxonomy of Computer Virus Defence Mechanisms'. Seven such mechanisms were highlighted (some of which have already been indicated):

- *message of notification*, signalling when a protected file is modified;

- *second copy and compare*, where a protected copy of the original of all files is used as a reference to determine whether contamination has occurred;

- *selected portions of programs*, allowing speedy comparisons (or more detailed comparisons) to be made;

- *length of program*, stored to allow a check on the length of a program to be performed (and so to detect modifications);

- *date/time stamp*, similar to program length check;

- *checksum*, allowing the program to be executed to be compared with the original (a strong encryption algorithm is recommended);

- *encryption*, to be used for all files to be stored (ideally, a virus trying to write to an encrypted program will produce only garbage).

Such measures may be expected to protect against many but not all attempts at virus penetration. Where a virus *has* managed to penetrate the security measures, it may be necessary to call in a virus expert, an effective 'system doctor'....

One such is Dr Alan Solomon, already met, who works for S&S Enterprises in Amersham, UK. The S&S service currently offers training about viruses, ensuring that a site is virus-free, and ridding sites of viruses when they are detected (one strategy is to write a 'hunter killer' virus that will spread through the same channels to detect and destroy the original virus). One procedure adopted by Solomon is to download the hard disk data to a Bernoulli box (a disk with removable cartridges), and then to reformat the disk. The floppy disks can then be tested using special software, after which all the clean floppies can then be write-protected with tabs.

Whatever measures are adopted (for virus prevention, detection or cure), it is clear that the situation is evolutionary: as new techniques are developed to counter the virus threat, new types of software are devised to circumvent the defensive measures. There will always be programmers and other specialist computer staff with an interest in stealing, challenging computer systems or simply having fun. Perhaps new legislation, in the UK and elsewhere, is needed to deter at least a proportion of such individuals.

In fact the first trial of a virus maker has already taken place. Donald Gene Burleson, once a highly regarded programmer at a large US brokerage and insurance firm, has been tried for sabotaging data, convicted, and sentenced to seven years' probation and ordered to pay back almost $12,000 to his former employer (the case is described in detail by Joyce, 1988).

The conviction took place under the 1985 Texas state computer sabotage law. Burleson was found guilty of infecting the computers of USPA & IRA, a Fort Worth company. Under the legislation he could have received two to ten years in jail and a fine of $5000, but was eligible for probation as a first-time offender. Company officials revealed during the trial that they had lost 168,000 records of sales commissions.

It was interesting that even at the time of his trial, Burleson had no problem with employment in the data processing industry. He was then working as a programmer at a Dallas telemarketing firm, though later dismissed when his picture appeared in a newspaper in connection with the trial. Asked, on the day he was sentenced, whether he intended to remain in the computer industry, he replied, 'I sure do'.

Anti-Virus Products

We are not surprised, in this hi-tech age, to encounter automated products designed to counter the virus threat. As soon as the first viruses were detected, various individuals and companies were quick to perceive a commercial niche. Writing of the various virus detection and protection products, Highland (1988) observed nicely: 'They are appearing as rapidly as toadstools on decaying wood after a rain storm.'

These products are software, often with (benign) virus characteristics, able to spread through a system to encounter viruses that have already made the same journey. Anti-virus products are now beginning to proliferate almost as fast as viruses. We cannot explore these in detail, but it is worth mentioning the following:

- **DPROTECT** is intended to write-protect floppy and hard disks, particularly against a Trojan horse;

- **Antigen** is designed to enable any program to perform its own virus detection every time the program runs;

- **VI-Raid** detects the presence of software in what is deemed virus-free software;

- **Antidote** is a virus filter for DOS operating systems microcomputers;

- **C-4** is a virus shield, reportedly tested using more than 1000 infected public-domain and commercial software packages;

- **Data Physician** protects a PC-DOS or MS-DOS computer system against viruses and logic bombs (Highland, 1987).

This listing is not intended to endorse any of the products: they are all relatively new, and testing of their claims is often far from complete. It is enough to note that there are now dozens, possibly hundreds, of such products and more are appearing all the time. We can also mention **Disk Defender, Disk Watcher, Flu Shot, Vaccine, Vaccinate, Viralarm, Immunize, Novirus** and **VirusSafe**. Most of these products originate in the US (details of companies and discussion of many of the products can be found in various issues of the journal *Computers and Security*).

SUMMARY

This chapter has discussed various aspects of computer

viruses, logic bombs, worms and Trojan horses. No attempt
has been made to provide a detailed technical insight into the
types of coding that enable viruses, for example, to reproduce
in computer systems and to achieve a wide range of unwelcome effects. The aim has been to provide an overview of virus
phenomena – their nature as a security threat, background
aspects, specific viruses and steps that may be taken to protect
against them.

Attention has also been given to the 'life metaphor' as a
fertile approach to characterising viruses and associated
phenomena. Here mention is made of the evolving 'life
characteristics' of (appropriately configured) computer systems, and there is particular focus on the extent to which the
epidemiological model can offer insights into how the security
of computer systems can be enhanced. Put another way, it is
feasible and useful to identify the computer analogues of
pathogens, vaccines, antibodies, etc. Knowledge of the immune system of human beings gives clues as to how security
provisions can be developed in computer systems.

Many security provisions are general, applying equally to
the protection of all aspects of computer systems; for example,
it is important to ensure that, as far as possible, staff are
competent and trustworthy. Basic security provisions of this
sort should be remembered when the question of the virus
threat is considered. In addition of course there are the
specific products and procedures being developed to address
specific types of threat. And again it is worth emphasising
that the threat is usually one step ahead of the remedy: the
protective measure is developed only after the threat is
perceived. This is as true for computer viruses as it is true for
other aspects of system security.

6 Social Impact

INTRODUCTION

New technology has always found ready uses in society, though at the same time viewed in a curiously ambivalent fashion. Technology can stimulate speculation and facilitate practical activity in the world, but it can also shatter cherished beliefs and undermine comfortable modes of existence. The advent of the computer caused structural changes in employment, sired new industries, and encouraged thought about psychology and other humanist topics. Attitudes to the computer are part of man's overall view of technology, and today it is easy to discern the traditional tensions and doubts. One observer, writing twenty years ago, suggested that attitudes to technology are much as they were a hundred years ago, but the tone 'is a bit shriller, more fearful, almost despairing at times' (Davenport, 1970).

Today there is proper anxiety about the impact of the computer; this does not gainsay its immensely valuable contribution in countless applications. What we see is a growing awareness that, as computers are given more powers in society, it is essential that they function in a reliable and secure way. There is a growing spectrum of applications in which computer failure poses a serious threat to human life. Computers, like any powerful tool, must be used in a controlled and intelligent way: we do no service to the development of computer technology if we countenance inappropriate applications or automated systems and procedures that are poorly designed, subject to functional failure or penetration by mischievous or malicious individuals.

We are accustomed to frequent collapses in technological systems (a few examples are given below): every week we read of failures in highly sophisticated artefacts. Engines fall off aircraft, bugs are encountered in commercial software, rockets fail to perform on test as predicted. In January 1989 an overloaded cable at Mercury Communications caught fire and hundreds of buildings in central London were thrown into darkness (Mercury was quoted: 'It was a new piece of cable which was protected by fuses which didn't blow, so it looks as if it was a cable fault'). And even when technology works as intended, there can be serious problems because of lack of human foresight (see Chapter 1). Joseph Weizenbaum, MIT guru, reckons that we are being swept along in a tide of 'technological inevitability', and he emphasises that serious problems can arise when computers are given tasks to perform that are far beyond their abilities. The Strategic Defence Initiative ('Star Wars') is regarded by many as a classic case in point (see Chapter 7).

It has been emphasised that computer-based systems can fail either through human incompetence or through deliberate human intervention. In fact all systems are prone to both categories of hazard; a poorly designed system, prone to failure, can also be tampered with, and in such a way the hazard is magnified. Indeed in many cases (eg during the early days of the enquiry into the Lockerbie air crash) we do not know whether a system collapse is due to design failure or sabotage. In any event we can stress again the need for reliable, secure computer systems in an increasingly automated world. This is particularly obvious when we consider the wide-ranging, multifaceted nature of the computer impact.

THE COMPUTER IMPACT

The impact of computers on developed and undeveloped countries is obvious to everyone (see also Chapter 1), and the main points do not need to be rehearsed here. We can however remind ourselves of the perennial (un)employment debate, a concern that is evident in 1989 and is sure to spin on through the 1990s. For example, in January 1989 a report from the UK National Audit Office suggested that more than 20,000 jobs in benefit offices must go over the next decade in order to keep the £1.7 billion computerisation of the social security system viable. At the same time it was noted that the costs for the computerisation programme had escalated while expected savings had more than halved.

This example highlights the anxiety that whereas computers have an undeniable impact on employment patterns (often generating new jobs as well as destroying old ones), costs are not always predicted accurately and development programmes can run into difficulty. At the end of 1988 the UK Commons Public Accounts Committee ordered Ministry of Defence planners to follow tough new guidelines on 'projects heavily dependent on software'. This follows such expensive matters as the cancellation of the Nimrod early warning system and the failure to develop certain command the control systems for navy frigates. It is obvious that military systems face particular hazards (see below and Chapter 7).

The computer impact sometimes has unexpected consequences. It has been argued that, for example, the UK national consumer credit debt of around £40 billion has largely arisen because of the sophisticated computer systems that speed up the assessment of a customer's credit worthiness. Such an assessment requires a rapid search through masses of personal information stored in computers. Banks, building societies and other organisations run their own credit evaluation systems. Philip Cooke, marketing director of the credit bureau Infolink, has argued that the current credit boom 'has been led at least in part by technology'. CCN and Infolink have 80 per cent of the UK market for credit references, with much of the rest being picked up by Westcot Data. CCN uses two Amdahl 5860 mainframe computers to store around 140 million records (including 44 million names from the electoral roll, 23 million postal addresses, 35 million records of previous credit searches and 100,000 fraud records).

The sheer scale of the personal information now stored

electronically invites many questions (which we can explore here). It is enough to remark that there are inevitably many mistakes in the records, and that inaccurate credit assessments can result from the way the databases are searched (for example, a search by the *address* of the application may mean that the applicant is judged by the credit record of someone else who once lived at the same address). Again we can emphasise that systems should be well designed and secure, a requirement that is difficult to meet in the context of a rapidly escalating use of databases for many different purposes (by the mid-1980s two UK government departments, the Home Office and the Department of Health and Social Security, held well over 100 million detailed personal records in about three dozen separate computer systems).

It is obvious that in development countries we are all affected, if only indirectly, by computer-based systems. Before profiling some areas where computer failures have been made dramatically obvious it is again worth glancing briefly at the key question of system vulnerability.

VULNERABILITY AND RISK

There are now many recorded cases of where system errors in computer-based facilities have resulted in inconvenience or hazard to human beings. For example, Wray (1988) instances fault lifts, chemical plants, lathes, guillotines, etc ('control systems based on computers are notoriously unpredictable'). It is stressed that much time and effort is spent, though not always successfully, on ensuring the safety of high-profile systems (such as air traffic, missile facilities and nuclear power plants); but that at least as much attention should be devoted to simpler systems that, because they are widespread, could in the event of failure threaten the lives of many people.

It can be an immensely difficult task to trace faults in computer software (see Bugs in Software, below), even in relatively small systems. And even where a system is technically sound (ie where it fully implements the original specification), it may invites calamity. Wray cites the case where, due to operator error, a computer 'tried to increase the temperature of a chemical process to 800 degrees Celcius when the operator meant only to achieve a pressure of 800 millimetres of mercury'. The resulting hazard – chemicals voided to the atmosphere – could have been prevented if the specification had stipulated temperature limits outside of which the system would have refused to act.

Dr John Cullyer, head of the Royal Signals and Radar Establishment's Safety Critical Department, has argued that computer-related deaths will start to rise alarmingly after 1992 – mainly in the nuclear, petrochemical and intelligent systems sectors where microprocessors are used to control dangerous processes ('The problem is due to the proliferation of safety critical systems. Up until now, they have been kept largely clear of the areas where they could cause harm to life'). Moreover it is suggested that the inevitable pressures of a competitive market are adding to the risks.

In the same vein, Dr David Clarke, an expert in medical computing, has spoken of a medical disaster looming – 'we have doctors untrained in the use of computer technology working on equipment they don't understand, which might not even be the right equipment in the first place' (quoted by Warren, 1988, in an article headed 'Killing Machines').

Such examples again highlight the need for effective systems design and for the best possible security provisions. The security expert Dr Ken Wong (of BIS Applied Systems) has emphasised that if a computer virus entered a program in a nuclear power station or chemical complex, 'it could wreak havoc'. And good design and security should aim to ensure the continuous availability of reliable, safe computer operations.

There is growing awareness of the 'increased dependence of enterprises on continuously operating computer systems' (Goyal and Lavenberg, 1987). This emphasises the need for 'fault-tolerant' designs. Martin (1987), for example, considers how the requirement for fault tolerance in network systems is moving the technology of network management towards the use of artificial intelligence. And this, in turn, raises the further question of accountability: who is liable if a wrongly-functioning expert system leads a company to financial loss, operational disaster or total collapse? The law bears on the question of risk, as do many other factors, but the position is often far from clear (see Problems in Law, below).

BUGS IN SOFTWARE

We may often suspect that a piece of software contains bugs but cannot be sure until they have observable effects. Sometimes the effects are inconsequential and can be tolerated; and sometimes, as we have seen, the effects can be catastrophic. Often the effects of bugs are neither inconsequential nor disastrous: costs are incurred, inconvenience is caused, and there may be far-reaching consequences for security measures and system development procedures.

A software fault in computers used by British Airways left the Babs reservation system out of action for a while in January 1989, with passengers and luggage having to be checked in manually. Technicians investigated the fault – which was thought to lie in a link between Babs and the BA-owned Travicom switching system. One possibility was a software bug, but an official declared: 'There is no logical reason for the problem.' At the same time Sun Microsystems were busy investigating user complaints about bugs in its newly-released operating system.

Version 4 of Sun's Unix-based operating system, SunOS, was available in the UK in June 1988, and soon users were protesting about faults in the software. Chris Brown, chairman of the Sun UK user group, who works at the Sheffield University research laboratory, has referred to 'a number of annoying bugs ... one of the reasons we haven't decided to upgrade to the new operating system' (quoted in *Computing*, 1 December 1988). Peter Rutter, Sun product marketing manager, has agreed that there are several 'minor bugs.... It is a major release. You expect to encounter a few'. It is in fact a common assumption that even small software systems will contain bugs, and that steps should be taken to weed these out or at least to contain them.

It is possible to trace the problems through the system-development life cycle. The specification, for instance, is required to accommodate the demands of a shifting environment: the system will have to deal with future, as well as current, requirements. It is easy to overlook circumstances that may occur in complex situations, such as chemical process plant. A typical program may contain thousands of lines of code, allowing many possible data values to be handled via many possible program paths. This situation yields a vast number of combinations, and it is impossible to check them all individually. Indeed the 'combinatorial explosion' is such that to check all the possibilities in even a relatively simple program would take an absurdly long time. Wray (1988) considers this approach for a 'relatively trivial' program and finds that if the necessary tests were carried out at the rate of 100 per second it would take 4×10^{24} years to complete them, ie a period many times the life of the Universe.

This suggests that it is impractical to fully test the vast majority of computer programs, and that they may therefore be assumed to contain bugs of various sorts. One estimate suggests that programmers typically introduce between 30 and 100 faults for every thousand lines of code written. Careful testing may reduce the figure to less than 10, but is not expected to remove all the bugs. This means that any process control program of around 20,000 lines will probably contain more than a hundred errors. It is impossible to detect these by comparison with the specification because the specification itself is likely to carry mistakes that have been faithfully coded in the subsequent program.

The developing situation in which untestable software is given increasing power in society is causing concern among many software experts. We have already cited Dr John Cullyer's concern about the probable increase in the number of computer-related deaths in the 1990s. In the same vein, Professor Manny Lehman, founder of Imperial Software Technology and an Emeritus Professor at Imperial College in London, has declared: 'I believe that the danger to mankind over the next 20 years from software pollution is greater than the danger from nuclear weapons' (quoted by Durham, 1988). A parallel is drawn with the 1930s when, Lehman suggests, nuclear physicists should have warned society about what they were doing.

The central argument is a familiar one. Software, even when judged to be 'correct', is not good enough for situations where a fault could cause serious harm. The world is complex and always changing: even adaptive software, with all possible safeguards, cannot necessarily accommodate all possible circumstances. By the time a program is used, there must inevitably be some implicit real-world assumptions that are no longer true 'and which, if invoked, could cause a disaster'. Lehman is particularly concerned about the claims being made for artificial intelligence, including expert systems. Even where software is designed to explain its reasoning, only the simplest inference chains could be followed by the human brain (some automated inference chains have thousands of steps).

Furthermore automated systems cannot necessarily be relied upon to out-perform human beings: the systems themselves, designed by men and women, will inevitably incorporate human errors. Lehman is enthusiastic about formal techniques as an important aid to the development of good-quality software, but such techniques are unable to address some of the crucial problems.

Various efforts are being made to protect people from the (possibly) bad effects of commercial software. Brian Oakley, chairman of the British Computer Society, has suggested that there is a danger that people will trust their expert systems, 'which may give an answer which is not necessarily true'; and he urges the need for professional guidelines that are akin to those used by organisations such as the British Medical Association (BMA). John Dawson, head of the BMA professional and scientific division, emphasises the need to control the use of powerful software. For example, the origin and date of the system development should be indicated on the software ('The guidance given in an expert system will reflect the underlying philosophy of the people who write it...').

However, whatever measures are taken to ensure that software is well designed and well coded, whatever ethical or legislative steps are taken to protect software users, the systems can never be assumed to be absolutely correct or the protection absolutely foolproof. Sometimes the problems are trivial; sometimes they are serious; and sometimes there is the potential for global disaster (see Chapter 7).

In January 1989 it was reported that the £1.2 billion UK Department of Social Security computerisation programme was being seriously hit by design faults and delays. For instance, faults have been revealed in systems designed for pensions and national insurance; in particular, the systems failed to deliver necessary information as planned. Managers blamed the failures on 'user inexperience and equipment failure'. It is said that programs used daily by benefit offices across the country still contain around one hundred known faults, despite efforts to remove them.

This is one example of many (others are given below) of where unexpected system failures have represented actual or potential hazards. The situation is likely to escalate unless it is addressed in a comprehensive and systematic fashion.

THE POLITICAL FRAME

There are many ways in which politics bears on the use of computer system (and most cannot be discussed here). We can think of the government use of computers at all levels of administration, social control, military provision, etc; relevant legislation (eg the 1984 Data Protection Act in the UK; and the growing use of computers in the democratic electoral process. This last category affords an important example of how computers are infiltrating the most important sociopolitical processes, but not always with the happiest results.

In the United States there is massive use of computers for vote tallying, a key democratic requirement that is at the heart of political legitimacy. If such computerised vote-tallying provisions are unreliable or open to fraud, then the democratic process is undermined. In fact there is accumulating evidence that such computer applications are far from satisfactory. In an important article, Roy Saltman (1988) provides excerpts from a 130-page report indicating potential inaccuracies and fraud in computerised voting systems. In one case (in Carroll County, Maryland: November, 1984), a computer declared the wrong person the winner of an election ('one of the computers used was in error in determining the outcome. . . .'). In 1985 a number of articles in the *New York Times* revealed that a computer program widely used for vote tallying was particularly vulnerable to fraud:

> 'The computer program that was used to count more than one-third of the votes cast in the Presidential election last year is very vulnerable to munipulation and fraud, according to expert witnesses in court actions challenging local and Congressional elections in three states . .' (*New York Times*, 29 July 1985)

In view of such observations and the evidence accumulated, it was concluded that there were problems in verifying election results, that undiscoverable fraud was a possibility, and that election administrators lack the necessary knowledge and resources.

In the Presidential election won by George Bush, more than 55 per cent of the votes cast were counted by computer systems, though it is well known by computer experts that the systems are prone to error and open to fraud. There is an abysmal lack of standards for such computer-based facilities. Often 'there is no audit trail, and no protection against computer viruses and rogue programs such as trapdoors, timebombs and Trojan horses that can secretly, and relatively easily, distort an election result' (Foremski, 1988). Today there are a number of court cases outstanding where fraud in computerised vote tallying systems is alleged.

Other political dimensions include: the extent to which Presidential campaigns have been effectively orchestrated by computer-run market research (see Perry's *The Programming of the President*, 1984); and the extent to which a computer virus could serve as a terrorist tool – 'just plant a virus and you can hold a whole country to ransom' (Shelton, 1988). We should also remember that astrologers sometimes use computers, and have influence over presidents.

COMPUTER ASTROLOGERS

In 1988 Donald T Regan, key White House insider (until forced to resign), revealed that Nancy Reagan had been using an astrologer's advice to influence the behaviour of President Ronald Reagan ('Nancy Reagan seemed to have absolute faith in the clairvoyant powers of this woman'). Particular dates were evaluated, according to astrological inside, as 'bad', 'very bad', 'be careful', 'no outside activity', 'no trips', etc; and the evaluations were used to help determine the presidential schedule of activity. Regan suggests that Nancy was the important believer in astrology, with Ronald prepared to agree to her wishes. Duncan Cambell, however, in almost identical articles in *Newstatesman and Society* (14 October 1988) and *Computer Talk* (14/27 November 1988), argues that Ronald Reagan has long been committed to astrology.

We need not pursue such eccentricities except to remark that the astrologers in question are apt to use computers, automated facilities that are subject to the usual software imperfections and security shortcomings.* Joan Quigley, Nancy's 'special friend', uses output from the DR70 micro-computer of another astrologer, Nicky Michaels, to assist her astrological evaluations.

AIRCRAFT SAFETY

Computer-based facilities are now commonplace in aircraft and air traffic control systems, and many anxieties are being expressed about this escalating level of automation. In short, how reliable are computers in circumstances where failure can result in fatalities?

In June 1988 an Airbus A320 crashed into a forest in Eastern France, killing three passengers. It was of immediate interest to journalists, technical pundits and others that the A320 uses automated flight controls, the 'fly-by-wire' techniques that replace mechanical controls with computers and electrical circuits. Extensive computerised monitoring is

*I refrain from speculating on what might have been the sociopolitical consequences of program bugs and computer viruses in software used to regulate the superstitions of an erstwhile American president.

designed to inhibit the effects of pilot actions if unsafe manoevres are attempted. The case remains controversial. The prompt statement by Mr Louis Mermaz, France's minister of transport, that there was nothing wrong with the aircraft – including, by implication, its computerised systems – did not convince all observers.

It has also been suggested that computerisation in aircraft cockpits can be confusing to pilots, particularly where the computerisation varies from one aircraft to another. For example, a Boeing sales pitch is that the same pilot can fly any of the 737 models, according to what the airline needs on a particular day. But Kenny Thomas, spokesman for the Airline Pilot's Association in Virginia, US, has stated that the differences in the complicated computerised cockpits of the three Boeing 737 models – including 737–400s similar to the British Midland jet that crashed by the M1 in the UK – are 'confusing to pilots'. (Captain Terry McKenna, a pilot with United Airlines, has observed that computerised displays do not always tell the pilot what the plane is doing – 'only what the computer thinks the plane is doing'.)

Air traffic control facilities in the UK continue to face problems associated with computers. In 1987 information on displays used at the Oceanic Air Traffic Control Centre at Prestwick in Scotland has been variously blacked out and overruled by staff because the information was perceived to be wrong. Computerised systems have failed, with staff forced to resort to manual procedures (a caption on a picture in *New Scientist*, 10 September 1987, reads: 'Controllers can't always rely on computers').

One problem seems to be bugs in the software supplied by Software Sciences, a subsidiary of Thorn EMI; and it has also been suggested that some design problems were not anticipated and slipped through the tests. Moreover the system has been forced to evolve as demands have increased – and this sort of situation is a sure, but unavoidable, recipe for difficulties. West Drayton, handling air traffic over England and Wales, has also experienced failures, as have air traffic control centres in Washington, Boston and elsewhere. 'A common feature of all these glitches is the failure of computer experts to predict how their complex software systems will behave after they have been written or amended' (Lamb, 1987).

The air traffic control system failed at Heathrow on 6th August 1988. Passengers were stranded, with controllers frantically telephoning around the country to learn the flight plans of aircraft in their charge. The Civil Aviation Authority decided that there was a software error in the system: in fact the old computer system needs dozens of full-time specialists to keep it working. Software changes are made every week – which introduce further bugs and cause further failures.

Use was made of the American-initiated National Airspace Package, and it was found to contain bugs from the start. One intriguing flaw was that, designed originally for the US environment, the package is not happy with a zero longitude: this caused the system to fold its map of Britain in two, confidently placing Norwich on top of Birmingham! Later system modifications (eg to allow connection to other computers) gave further scope for bugs.

The Civil Aviation Authority is installing a new IBM-based flight control system at Heathrow in 1989. It is hoped that the four IBM 4381 computers will be more reliable than the current IBM 9020D, but with air traffic increasing at nearly 10% a year there will certainly be more congestion. It is likely that the traditional system problems will afflict the new facilities, designed as they are to cope with highly complex data in a rapidly changing environment. Over the past eighteen months there have been about half a dozen computer breakdowns at West Drayton, and no less than nineteen in new Oceanic ATC systems at Prestwick. It is interesting that the new IBM systems at West Drayton will use software that is much the software employed for traffic control in the early-1970s. Today this software has been described as 'a jumble of poorly maintained code' (Lawrence, 1988). Steve Hall of the Guild of Air Traffic Controllers has declared that 'most of the failures have been software'.

It is claimed that so far none of the failures has proved

dangerous, but it is also true that the systems (and maintenance personnel) will be put under increasing pressure in the
years ahead. By 1989 there was obvious concern about the
number of aircraft 'near hits', a problem that is unlikely to go
away with massively increased air traffic in the years ahead.

HEALTH AND HOSPITALS

The growing use of computers in hospitals and other health-
care institutions is inevitably associated with a number of
software-linked accidents. For instance, David Clarke,
already mentioned, has remarked that *'There have already
been cases in the US and Europe where people have been fried
during X-ray scanning therapy because of errors in computer
programs'* (my italics). Joyce (1987) gives details of cases
concerning a computerised therapeutic radiation machine
now thought to be implicated in the deaths of two patients and
serious injuries to several others.

In one case Voyne Ray Cox was given radiation treatment
in March 1986. When the radiation machine was turned on by
a technician, Cox experienced a severe pain in his shoulder
and heard a frying sound; a further burst of 'treatment'
caused him to roll across the table; and after a third burst of
radiation he jumped off the table and called for help.
Inspection revealed a machine Malfunction 54 which had
switched off the equipment. Too late – before long, Cox was
vomiting blood and much of his body was paralysed. He lapsed
into a coma and died in a Dallas hospital six months later.

The same equipment, the Therac 25 unit, was thought to be
implicated in the death in 1986 of Verdon Kidd in Texas;
another patient, Caty Yarbrough, was given a radiation
overdose in Marietta, Georgia. Joyce suggests that such cases
will raise the 'risk consciousness' of the computer industry.
Susan Nycum, one of the lawyers in the Therac case, has
declared: 'It's a horrible tragedy, but I don't think very many
computer experts are really surprised. After all, *software's
written by people and people make mistakes*' (my italics).

Computers have also been condemned as likely to lead to
divers getting decompression sickness (the 'bends'). Royal

Navy diving experts have acquainted officials of the British Sub-Aqua Club with their concern (but the officials, with a financial interest in the supplier company, continued to recommend the machines).

The objections focus on the fact that the wrist-strap computers, designed to tell divers how slowly they should ascend to avoid the bends, take no account of such crucial factors as age, fitness and sex (and so can mislead the diver). Surgeon Captain Ramsey Pearson, head of undersea medicine at the Institute for Naval Medicine in Gosport, Hampshire, pointed out (in October 1988) that 34 of 80 cases of decompression sickness dealt with at the institute during the year involved computers. It is estimated that around 5000 of Britain's 50,000 divers now use wrist computers. One diver of 18 years' experience, Van der Boon, blames a computer for his attack of the bends ('If there had been the slightest whisper from the national office about any problems, then I would not have got the bends. Now I only use the computer as a back-up'). The supplier, the Swiss firm Uwater that makes the Aladin wrist computer, has rejected all allegations that the device might be unsafe.

There are of course many other health problems associated with the use of computer-based facilities. We need only mention stress (Wagenaar, 1985), backstrain, headaches, eyestrain, foetal malformation and spontaneous abortion. The evidence for many such supposed causal links is often highly suspect, but it is true that many of the questions remain unresolved. There is no room for complacency about the effect of computer usage on human health.

WEATHER PREDICTION

Meteorology is another field in which computers are finding a growing range of applications, and in which successful prediction (eg of extreme weather conditions) can be important to human safety. For instance, the 'hurricane' that hit England in October 1987 led to the deaths of nineteen people, uprooted 15 million trees, and caused £1 billion worth of damage. That the country was not forewarned was attributed in part to poor computer performance.

The British Meteorological Office failed to anticipate events because the various computer forecasts were 'unusually confusing' and contradictory. The culprit was a Control Data Cyber 205 supercomputer, capable of 400 million calculations a second and of producing a 24-hour world weather forecast at fifteen altitude levels in less than five minutes. Unfortunately it predicated showers and light winds for England, while anticipating storms 80 miles east in the North Sea. One of the Cyber's operators observed that it was difficult to know what had gone wrong ('It's possible that a small piece of information got into the computer which shouldn't have'). And the Met Office advised staff to be ready to rely on their own personal judgement if they suspected that the prevailing weather conditions were beyond the scope of their technology.

THE PREJUDICED COMPUTER

In early-1988 it was revealed that a computer used to select students had been running racially and sexually prejudiced software. A selection program used at St George's medical school, south London, deliberately downgraded non-whites and women. Candidates were classified as Caucasian or non-Caucasian on the basis of their names and their photographs, if available; and were classified on the basis of their sex. A candidate could lose 15 points for being non-white and three points for being female.

An investigating commission estimated that about sixty candidates a year were being deprived of interviews for which they should have qualified. It was suggested that the program merely enshrined existing prejudice. After exposure in November 1986, the program was scrapped – but by then it had been running for four years.

Here the point is a simple one. There is no suggestion that the computer system was malfunctioning or open to security penetration (though this was almost certainly the case). What is important was that individuals, possibly unaware of how the software was weighted, were encouraged to place undue reliance on computer deliberations. This is a common condition when people are confronted with computer-based facilities. Thus it is not sufficient that systems be functionally reliable and adequately protected. It is also necessary that the real-world assumptions on which they are based are sound and open to scrutiny.

MILITARY SYSTEMS

Today there are many ways in which computers can become involved in the business of war. They can, for example:

- play war games, as a method of testing strategic options;

- provide weapons (tanks, aircraft, ships, missiles, etc) with decision-making capabilities, a modicum of intelligence;

- monitor the shifting world political scene as relevant to the likelihood of war at any particular time;

- take the decisions (on missile launches, etc) that start a war or respond to aggression.

We do not need to discuss these points in detail: aspects of military computing have been considered in Chapter 1, and the Strategic Defence Initiative is discussed in Chapter 7. Here it is enough to highlight a few obvious conclusions:

- war games, as highly simplified representations of reality, are unreliable and misleading;

- military networks are insecure to a greater or lesser extent, as shown by various system penetrations through the 1980s (for example, in 1984 two teenage hackers broke into the secret ARPA network used by the Pentagon; in 1988 thousands of military computers are affected by the Internet virus – see Chapter 5);

- military computing systems, because of their complexity and inadequate evolutionary capabilities, are unreliable to a greater or lesser extent. Failures of the Wimex computers at the North American Air Defence (NORAD) headquarters are now well known. US nuclear forces have been wrongly put on war alert at least three times.

Nuclear alerts have been caused by loading a wrong tape
onto a computer, and by the failure of a $20 silicon chip.

Computers in military systems, like computers elsewhere,
are subject to the usual problems associated with reliability
and security. There is, however, a further dimension: the most
powerful computerised weapons systems can never be fully
tested in the real world, except in the most appalling
circumstances. Nor can it be known for certain that the
current operational systems are working with adequate
reliability and security (the available morsels of evidence
suggest a pessimistic interpretation). It is clear that the
consequences of computer failure in the military domain are
the gravest we can imagine.

PROBLEMS IN LAW

The law offers some protection against the unwelcome social
consequences of computer failure, for whatever reason. Companies may contract for contingency provision or may take
out legally recognised insurance cover. But there are many
problems associated with legal protection. For example, the
question of damages when someone has been sold defective
software is still a matter of debate (Staines, 1987), and
worries about litigation can act as a confusing brake on the
development of computer applications (Warner, 1988 – 'No-
where is the concern over product liability stronger than
among companies working on expert systems for medical
applications, where malpractice suits already abound').

It is anticipated that expert systems, for example, will be
increasingly used in the corporate sector; but their use is
certain to be affected by product-liability litigation in the US.
One reason why this form of litigation has escalated 'is the
increasing number of lawyers who specialise in computer-
related issues' (Warner). Darrel Ince, in a wide-ranging
article (1988), explains how 'legal cases involving new
technology are causing headaches to judges the world over'.
The ubiquitous social impact of computers is signalled today
by many factors – from technophobia to structural changes in
employment, from increasing awareness of ethical concerns

(Speller and Brandon, 1986; Cohen, 1988) to pressure for legislative change.

SUMMARY

This chapter has charted some of the reasons for the growing concern about the developing social impact of computers. The nature of the social impact is briefly indicated (as a supplement to the more detailed discussion in Chapter 1). Questions of system vulnerability, risk and software bugs are explored in the context of increasing social reliance on computer-based facilities (Tate, 1988 – 'Organisations have become dependent on IS systems for their survival'). Then particular examples of computer failure, associated with hazards to human beings, are indicated.

The relevance of increased computerisation to political matters is considered, with emphasis here on possible threats to the democratic process. Then brief details are given of concern about the use of computers in aircraft and air traffic control; in health matters, weather prediction, student selection, and military activities. The relevance of law (and of increasing ethical awareness) in the context of a rapidly changing technology is emphasised.

The main theme of the chapter is that computer-based systems, given functional responsibility in important areas, can represent hazards to human beings in various ways. It is not enough, moreover, that computer systems be reliable (eg free from bugs) and secure (eg immune to penetration). They must also enshrine sound assumptions about the real world in general and people in particular. It is important that the assumptions underlying software – particularly where such assumptions involve value judgements about human beings – are known to the users and open to scrutiny at any time. There can, however, be immense difficulties in making such assumptions explicit, if only because they are so numerous.

This suggests that computer systems that are given power over people's lives should be examined with great care, treated with great caution, viewed with circumspection. Computer software should not be regarded as a foolproof way of avoiding human fallibility; but as a complex class of artefacts able to enshrine human error in new and unexpected ways. It is the business of the software engineer, at least in part, to ensure that computer systems represent as little hazard as possible to human beings in society. All artefacts are imperfect; imperfect artefacts with power over human lives can be dangerous creatures.*

*Tom Forester, in a fascinating article (*Computer Talk*, May 22–June 4, 1989, pp 12–13), discusses some of the trivial and serious consequences that have resulted from computer faults. They include: restaurant diners ordering trout and being served octopus; the UK National Health Service inviting men to attend for cervical screening; the downing of the Korean Air Lines flight 007; suppression of crucial data about damage to the ozone layer; disenfranchising of electors in Brazil; destruction of a US Atlas-Agena rocket; US cat owners asked to register their dachshunds; a West German woman, wrongly told she had passed syphilis to her offspring, killing her daughter; a US woman wrongly imprisoned; a US man wrongly arrested five times; an insurance computer making $60 million overpayments; 18 million litres of sewage fed into a river . . .

7 Star Wars

INTRODUCTION

The concept of the Strategic Defence Initiative (SDI or 'Star Wars') is, in some ways, a paradigm of ambitious computerisation. SDI relies upon the successful exploitation of several co-operating technologies where computer-based systems play a central part. In particular, SDI uses computers, communication links (with artificial satellites), lasers and sensors to establish what purports to be a defensive 'umbrella' against Soviet nuclear missiles. In fact there is as yet no deployed SDI system. The many contributing elements are currently being researched in the United States and elsewhere, and there are signs that President Bush is less committed to the SDI project than was Ronald Reagan. Moreover the problem of the US budgetary deficit will probably put pressure on the new administration to reduce SDI expenditure below the original vastly expensive levels.

It is worth highlighting three of the general principles advanced by advocates of SDI:

- it is practical to design a highly complex computer system that, though never fully tested, will perform reliably when necessary in a rapidly changing real-world situation;

- it is justified to grant such a system a degree of decision-making autonomy, in view of the advantages of rapid machine response over the relatively tardy responses of human beings;

– it is justified to give computer-based facilities immense power in a domain that involves not merely the lives of a few hundred people (as, for example, in a modern airliner) but, arguably, the survival of the human race.

Some of these points are considered in the present chapter. A main purpose is to profile the SDI concept, to highlight background aspects, and to indicate some of the doubts and anxieties regarding any plan to deploy an SDI system in the years ahead. We will see that the main concern is *whether a massively complicated system, run by computers, can be expected to work reliably and securely in a dynamic and (possibly) hostile environment.*

Little attention is given to such questions as whether SDI is truly defensive (an effective shield gives more power to one's sword, and, in any case, lasers on space platforms could in theory be directed at any desired target, including terrestrial cities). Such a political question cannot be pursued here but it should be remembered that political interest can encourage individuals – politicians, journalists, military personnel, systems experts, etc – to support particular views regarding the prospects of system reliability and system security.

BACKGROUND

All the technologies that were to combine in the SDI concept had their origins many years before Ronald Reagan came to power. Artificial satellite systems were well established, important work on lasers was carried out in the 1960s (with various laser and beam weapons emerging in the early-1970s, carrying names such a Sipapu, Chair Heritage and White Horse), and the key computational and communications technologies were continuing to build on the dramatic developments that had occurred in the 1960s and 1970s.

Soon after Reagan was elected US President in January 1981, he became involved in talks that were to lead to SDI. Edward Teller, 'father of the H-bomb', was already an enthusiastic proponent of the nuclear-pumped, X-ray laser; and he recommended an ideological ally, George Keyworth, as the President's science advisor. Already the Pentagon had spent vast sums on a number of projects that were relevant to SDI.

Meetings were held at the Heritage Foundation in Washington DC by people (scientists, industrialists and others) committed, for whatever reason, to an antimissile programme. Individuals, including Pentagon officials, organised an effective lobby for further development of the various projects – nuclear X-ray lasers, kinetic impact weapons, bean devices, etc – underway at the Livermore and other research establishments in the US. A group from the Heritage Foundation first met Reagan in January 1982, and Teller had further private meetings. By now the secret work had spread to many aspects: nuclear bomb driven X-ray lasers, orbiting kill satellites, monitor satellites to survey the Soviet Union, ground-based lasers, space mirrors, satellite beam weapons, etc. No component of SDI had yet been proven, much less deployed; and it was now clear that the escalating costs could no longer be contained in secret budgets. Reagan decided to go public.

In March 1983 President Reagan announced the Strategic Defence Initiative as a 'means of rendering the ballistic missile threat impotent and obsolete'. James Fletcher, a previous administrator of NASA, led a technology study of how the missile defence strategy might work; and General James Abrahamson was appointed head of the new SDI Office set up by the White House. The SDI programme was given $1400 million in its first full budget for the 1985 financial year, an amount said to be somewhat less than what was spent on laser and beam weapons in 1984. Between 1985 and 1989, the US Department of Defence requested $26 billion for SDI projects (and usually received about 60 per cent of what was asked for). The SDI concept had become enshrined in US technology research and military thinking. Despite many expert criticisms (see Some Objections, below), powerful sectors in the US had combined to sustain the programme. David Baker, a NASA consultant for twelve years, commented: 'the programme that began so long ago had survived greater challenges than all its opponents could mobilise. It had been shown to be bigger than the highest office in the

land and would not go away. It is most unlikely that it ever
will' (Baker, 1987).

The momentum of SDI derives in part from the sheer scale
of the programme. In the mid-1980s, around 150 military
projects were placed under the control of the Strategic
Defence Initiative Organisation (SDIO). It was realised that
many different technologies would have to combine to render
SDI a viable option. For example, SDI research was soon
focusing on developments in high-speed integrated circuits
and in non-silicon substances (eg gallium arsenide) for
solid-state electronics. It was also necessary to research
systems design, communications protocols, and procedures in
software engineering. Some critics were already suggesting
that the software problems would prove to be intractable.
*How could software be produced to control the unimaginably
complex sensing, communications and resource allocation data
in the unpredictably chaotic conditions of nuclear war?*

Despite the on-going scientific and political commitment to
SDI, its history is nonetheless marked by shifting goals and
ambitions – brought about by a growing awareness of the
massive difficulties involved in achieving an operational SDI
system. The Pentagon is now saying that SDI will not provide
complete protection against nuclear missiles, and some of the
early enthusiasm for the concept has waned. John Pike,
Associate Director for Space Policy of the Federation of
American Scientists, has declared that since Reagan's 1983
speech 'much of the technical "progress" had consisted of
reducing support for unpromising technologies' (Pike, 1988).
And many of the tests of SDI have, to date, been less than
impressive. For example, a laser (the MIRACL, Mid-Infrared
Advanced Chemical Laser) was set up to destroy a grounded
Titan booster; and a Delta 181 rocket, launched in 1988, was
able to collect data on post-boost vehicles, warheads and
decoys – both tests being a far cry from demonstrating the
practicality of destroying vast numbers of nuclear missiles in
flight.

Many problems have been encountered in the multifaceted
SDI research and development programme. Pike has high-

lighted a number of examples:

- the Airborne Optical Adjunct project, designed to enable a Boeing 767 aircraft to carry a telescope for monitoring enemy warheads is a year behind schedule, and costs have escalated;

- a fire in the test chamber of the Alpha chemical laser caused a delay of six months in testing;

- the Relay Mirror Experiment, originally scheduled for 1988, is now expected to take place some time in 1989;

- plans for 3000 satellites, each carrying a dozen interceptors, have now been scaled down to between 150 and 300 satellites;

- the first test of the High-Endoatmosphere Defence Interceptor (HEDI), intended to destroy Soviet warheads, failed when the rocket sled carrying the prototype jumped its track, destroying the equipment.

In 1987 the then US Secretary of Defence, Frank Carlucci, urged the phased introduction of an SDI facility. The initial phase, beginning in the late-1990s, would be restricted to military targets: the civilian population would not, at that time, be defended by any SDI systems. This is not of course what was claimed for SDI in the heady days of 1983/84.

However, it is important to appreciate that even if the original fanciful SDI concept is not realised in full, it is inevitable that the on-going research will feed into fresh military systems. It is already being suggested that particular SDI projects can be translated into non-SDI programmes that have a better chance of success. And, for the purposes of the present book, it is significant that many such programmes will depend upon the development of effective computer-based facilities. This means that the perennial problems of program bugs, system reliability and system security will be of central importance in any SDI-linked systems, whether or not the emerging systems are faithful to the original SDI concept.

Aspects of systems reliability and system security are considered below. In this context, criticisms of SDI (see Some

Objections) have clear relevance to any large computer-based systems. This is of particular concern in the military area. Again we can stress that SDI can serve as a nice paradigm of systems that are given autonomy in war initiation and war management. It is useful to give a brief profile of what the SDI concept entails, with particular attention to 'launch-on-warning', the feature that is intended to provide a crucial element of system autonomy in response to perceived (ie artificially sensed) aggression.

PROFILE

The original SDI concept suggested that it was realistic to develop a defensive 'umbrella' – comprising massive computerisation, a global communications network (including artificial satellites), laser weapons, vast space-sited mirrors, etc – that would prevent any Soviet nuclear missiles from reaching the mainland of the United States in the event of war. (In eccentric moments President Reagan remarked that once the SDI technology had been developed it would be offered to the Russians. No-one took this seriously.)

A main SDI theme was that a three-layered defensive 'shield' would be put in place, with beam weapons designed to operate in the first layer. The high-energy beam weapons, using lasers, would be land-or space-based. It was also suggested that mirrors would be launched when an early-warning satellite signalled that a missile attack was imminent (though it is hard to see how such a launch would not involve unacceptable delays in SDI response to the perceived attack).

Once in space, the mirrors would be correctly positioned so that laser beams transmitted from the ground could be reflected at ballistic missiles once they had left the atmosphere. In an alternate configuration, space-based lasers would commence firing as soon as the appropriate warnings were received from the orbiting satellites or from other systems able to detect the imminent threat. Whichever configuration is in place, the aim is to destroy the intercontinental ballistic missiles soon after they are launched.

The first layer of defence works on the assumption that it is relatively easy to detect ballistic missiles during their boost phase: infra-red and other types of sensors can be designed to detect rocket plumes (and, hopefully, to ignore other heat sources – car engines, power plants, forest fires etc). It is obviously helpful to destroy a missile during its boost phase since it is still carrying all of its warheads. It is also harder because little time is allowed for detection, response and destruction. An attack on a ballistic missile during boost is, where successful, particularly effective: the unused volume of fuel makes the missile very vulnerable. Another 'first-layer' possibility is that satellites, permanently armed with missiles, could respond as soon as a warning was received. This 'launch-on-warning' concept (see below) is of particular importance in connection with the decision-making capabilities of modern military computers.

It may be that some ballistic missiles penetrate the first defensive layer (even SDI advocates admit that this is likely). A second layer is intended to comprise ground-launched missiles that would try to intercept incoming missiles that had escaped the laser beams or the satellite-launched missiles. Again use would be made of infra-red and other sensors that would be designed to track incoming nuclear warheads. And a third layer of defence would try to intercept any warheads that survived the first two defensive shields.

It is obvious that many elements would be necessary to give a deployed SDI system any chance of success. Thousands of sensors would be carried in (orbiting and geostationary) satellites, in ground stations, in aircraft and ships, etc. The hundreds of satellites, ground-stations, missile sites, laser systems, orbiting mirrors and the rest would be linked in a vast communications system that would ring the globe. The data to be handled by the entire configuration would be prodigiously diverse and unimaginably complex. As with any large computer system, the various modes, elements, components, etc would be established in a piecemeal fashion. No single human being could possibly understand the entire system in depth.

The SDI computers would necessarily have immense pow-

ers. They would need, for example, the capacity to discrimin-
ate between sound and unsound sensor information. (Was
that *really* a missile plume, or perhaps a burning chemical
plant? Indeed, was there *any* real-world activity to monitor, or
was the sensor malfunctioning?)

Once the computers had decided that the sensor data truly
signalled an imminent missile attack, they would first need to
orchestrate a highly complex response involving nuclear
explosions, laser transmissions, mirror launchings, mirror
positionings, missile firings, etc; and, in supervising 'second-
layer' defence, to distinguish between thousands of dangerous
missiles and tens of thousands of decoys (these latter deliberately designed to confuse sensors, to encourage computers to
process irrelevant and misleading data).

The computers would need to calculate the trajectories of all
the projectiles deemed to be threatening. Some missiles may
be targeted on satellites; others may be designed to destroy
interceptors launched from satellites or from the ground. The
computers would need to know what to do in every case: and
this includes knowing how to respond in situations that could
never have been imagined by the human system designers
and programmers. It would also be necessary for the computers to 'pool' their knowledge – so that a comprehensive view
of the escalating battle scenario was maintained; and for
them to interpret the vast quantities of incoming data so that
the enemy's strategy could be identified. Perhaps the pre-
liminary attack is a mere skirmish designed to exhaust SDI,
after which a crushing blow is dealt through a largely
ineffectual shield. Can the computers regulate the deployment of resources in order to repel a second wave of missile
attacks, a third, a fourth . . .?

It is obvious that the computers would have to perform
thousands of millions of calculations every second – flawlessly, using largely untried software in unprecedented battle
conditions. The massive volume of computation, involving a
prodigious mass of decision making every second, would have
to be carried out automatically: no human being, or human
group, could be allowed into the operational loops responsible

for data handling in a massively complex battle scenario that was changing by the second. There can be no doubt that the SDI war will be fought by machines, but machines will not be the only casualties.

The need for speedy and automatic response begins when the first missile plumes are detected: as soon as an imminent attack is perceived it will be necessary for the appropriate SDI systems to spring into action. One key aspect of this initial response – 'launch on warning' – deserves a separate mention.

LAUNCH ON WARNING

If a country is about to be attacked by nuclear missiles, it had better do something about it – and quickly. This is the simple (and understandable) rationale behind the 'launch on warning' concept. It involves allowing computers to launch retaliatory missiles in response to sensor indication of imminent attack. The aim can be either to destroy the incoming missiles or to make an unacceptable nuclear strike against the aggressor country.

The alternative may be to do nothing until the results of the attack are clearly known. Once the attack is over, decisions can be made about the form that the retaliation should take – if, of course, there is anyone left to make decisions. In fact, military strategists seem to have little enthusiasm for 'riding out' nuclear attacks: it is much better, they tend to argue, to strike back while you have the chance. This means *launch-on-warning*, and launch-on-warning means giving computers an important element of autonomy in the war-making situation.

Any launch-on-warning system demands an impressively capable computer system. Sensor data must be processed very quickly and launch data fed to lasers and/or missiles. It is essential that the response be rapid, that its effects (destroying enemy missiles, achieving airborne missiles heading for enemy territory, etc) are accomplished before the enemy strike occurs; and the necessary speed of response clearly precludes any *human* involvement.

It is also important that the computer systems are reliable:

a 'retaliatory' strike against a non-existent imminent attack would be deeply unpopular. And again we can consider the perennial topics that plague software engineers and system users – bugs, system reliability, risk, system security, etc (and see below).

The increased accuracy of modern missiles gives countries an interest in launch-on-warning. If incoming missiles are accurate enough to destroy missile sites, them there may be no opportunity for retaliation. Better to get the missiles into the air while there's still a chance!

In an interesting survey of options in this area, Borning (1987) indicates some of the disparate attitudes to launch-on-warning. One possibility is to launch missiles unarmed, and for arming to be accomplished via an encrypted command while the missiles are in flight. This would allow more time for fateful decisions, and perhaps a human being or two could be allowed into the decision-making loop. Alternatively, armed missiles could be *dis*armed in flight. It has to be said, however, that such options are not in the mainstream of SDI discussion.

Soviet attitudes to launch-on-warning receive little publicity, even in the age of glasnost. The former Soviet Defence Minister, Dmitri Ustinov, denied in 1983 that the Soviets intended to adopt a launch-on-warning strategy; but perhaps, with a new Defence Minister and newly-accurate US Pershing missiles, attitudes have changed.

The question of computer reliability has always made it difficult to support unambiguously a launch-on-warning posture (even if there were not other reasons for hesitation). At the same time many military strategists (Boring cites General Ellis of the Strategic Air Command, and General Herres, commander in chief, NORAD) are keen to retain launch-on-warning as a military option. Borning argues that it is not responsible of governments to support launch-on-warning strategies ('there is considerable doubt that adequate reliability can be achieved'), not least because of the enormity of system failure ('The standard of reliability required of a military system that can potentially help precipitate a thermonuclear war if it fails must be higher than that of *any* other computer system, since the magnitude to disaster is so great'). However, we have seen that the necessary levels of system reliability – involving both an absence of design and programming faults, and security against mischievous or malicious penetration – are not easily achieved.

BUGS AND RELIABILITY

Not all SDI reliability problems relate to computer software. We have already mentioned, for example, a rocket-driven sled that jumped off its tracks. Another case concerns the testing of an SDI solid-fuel rocket propellant that exploded at the headquarters of Aerojet General, a leading SDI contractor. In this accident one engineer was killed and one injured. This unfortunate event, which occured in August 1986, was one of several accidents that had dogged the American space effort.

Part of the problem is that complex systems are apt to sometimes behave in unpredictable ways – though system design or construction faults, or because particular circumstances had not been envisaged. This is particularly true of computer configurations, the most complex (non-biological) systems of all. We have already indicated (in Chapter 2) the various ways in which systems can go wrong, and we have repeatedly emphasised the impossibility of guaranteeing totally correct (ie totally bug-free) computer software. Again it is worth emphasising such matters in connection with SDI development; for example, in connection with launch-on-warning. Thomas J Watson, head of IBM, had commented that: 'as machines of war and missiles become more prey to pre-emptive strike, the more temptation there is to put more and more data in the hands of the computer and take the human being out of the equation.' And so, 'to the extent that you do that, you are indeed putting the US in a position where a computer could trip us up pretty badly' (*Computerworld*, 15 June 1983, p 15). In this context we could be 'tripped up' by program bugs or by inadequate computer security.

The Strategic Defence Initiative Organisation (SDIO) convened the Panel on Computing in Support of Battle Management. On 28 June 1985, David Lorge Parnas, a respected computer scientist, resigned from the Panel. Eight short essays on why he thought that the SDI software would inevitably be untrustworthy accompanied his letter of resignation. These essays have been widely published: they can be found in, for example, Parnas(1985).

The essays cover:

- the differences between software engineering and other forms of engineering, and why software is unreliable;
- why the proposed SDI software is unattainable;
- why the techniques used to build military software are inadequate;
- why software engineering cannot produce a truly reliable SDI system;
- why artificial intelligence will not help in building reliable military software;
- why research in automatic programming will not substantially improve matters;
- why program verification (using mathematical proofs of correctness) cannot provide reliable SDI systems;
- why military funding of computer science is inefficient and ineffective.

Parnas points out that, significantly enough, software products often carry specific disclaimers of warranty. Even the 'most competent programmers in the world cannot avoid' the problems associated with software failure. Moreover it is impossible to use program verification (mathematical proof) methods in the SDI context:

'It is inconceivable to me that one could provide a convincing proof of correctness of even a small portion of the SDI software. Given our inability to specify the requirements of the software, I do not know what such a proof would mean if I had it.'

If it is impossible to frame an adequate requirements

specification (since the exact battle conditions will not be known until they occur) and equally impossible to test the SDI system in any comprehensive way, then it is difficult to see how anyone could have confidence in the deployment of even a scaled-down version of SDI. And again we can emphasis the inevitability of a large number of program bugs in any massive piece of software (and SDI would be the largest chunk of software ever attempted).

We have seen that program errors can be introduced at any stage of the system development life cycle. Testing, where possible, will expose some faults, but corrective reprogramming will introduce more. It will then be found, particularly in the case of SDI, that the problem scenario has changed (with new developments in military technology) and so the requirements specification, already inadequate, is rapidly becoming totally irrelevant. Even a totally faithful coding of the specification would yield a system that had an ever diminishing relationship to the real world; and, as we have observed, such fidelity is never achieved.

There are various estimates of the likely number of bugs in the delivered code. We suggested (in Chapter 6) that typical estimates suggested between 30 and 100 faults in every thousand lines, with testing able, in propitious circumstances, to reduce the number to less than ten. In a highly regarded book, Boehm (1981) indicates that errors were found to range from 30 to 85 per thousand delivered source instructions. The actual number in any project, will be determined by the nature of the application, the competence of the programmer(s) and what counts as an error. Dennis Fife, of the US National Bureau of Standards, has stated that there are about 3.3 faults per thousand in software for large systems.

A system developed and maintained by Bell Communications Research, and comprising two million lines, had exhibited a range of 0.8 to 1.3 defects per thousand lines of new source code on three releases per year over a four-year period. T R Thomsen, president of AT&T Technology Systems, has indicated an error incidence of 0.5 to 3.0 occurrences per 1000 lines of program. (Both these examples are cited by Myres, 1986.)

It has also been suggested (eg by Putman et al, 1985) that the number of faults per thousand lines of code increases exponentially with the size of the system. Estimates of the size of the SDI Software range from 10 million to 100 million lines of code. Thus a best-case estimate of the number of faults in the SDI system would suggest around 5000 bugs at the time the system became operational (and this allows nothing for exponential increase with complexity). Myers, in common with most other observers, concludes that the SDI shield, if ever deployed will contain errors 'and the shield will leak – perhaps only a few warheads, but leaks nonetheless'.

At best, the SDI system will only provide a partial defence. And so far we have said nothing about the possibility of system penetration by virus makers and other mischievous or malicious agents.

VULNERABILITY

Most of the critical literature devoted to SDI focuses on whether system faults can be avoided when designers and programmers work with the 'best possible' intentions. It is acknowledged that the requirements specification may not cope adequately with an enemy who refuses to co-operate, but there has been relatively little attempt to discuss the consequences of mischievous programmers, inside or outside the SDI project, who work with the 'worst possible' intentions. In short, a small proportion of the 'inside' programmers may be tempted to plant Trojan horses; and some 'outside' programmers, for political or other reasons, may try to insert computer viruses into the system. These possibilities highlight many of the traditional security concerns.

The Internet virus (see Chapter 5) – which in 1988 showed how easily military systems could be penetrated – raised the spectre of an insecure SDI complex able to 'launch on warning'. Thus an item in *Computing* (17 November 1988) includes the observation that the Iternet virus 'has raised serious questions about the vulnerability of the Strategic Defence Initiative'. And, in this vein, a celebrated 'hacker tracker', Brian K Reid, has also expressed worries about SDI's vulnerability: 'I'm pretty good at breaking into computer systems – I can pretty much get into anything I want. And I'm passably confident that, if I had time and the financial backing to get the necessary radio links, I could probably break into SDI once they built it... Somewhere there's got to be a Russian who's as good as I am' (quoted by Frenkel, 1987).

SOME OBJECTIONS

We have already indicated the typical objections to the SDI project, and there is no need to rehearse the points in detail. However it is important to remind ourselves of the weight of technical opinion that is critical of the broad SDI concept (and this leaves out any *political* objections that may be made in the age of glasnost).

Professor Wiezenbaum of MIT, concerned at the possible misuses of computer power, has stated: 'I believe with Parnas and many others, that the software required simply cannot be produced to the degree of confidence without which is would be a meaningless exercise.' Larry Smart, head of a supercomputer unit at the University of Illinois, is one of hundreds of scientists (including computer specialists) who have refused to work on SDI because it is technically suspect ('... there is no way you could produce code large enough to handle the job and do it perfectly the first time, which is what you would need. I can't imagine any developments in computer technology that would make it possible in the foreseeable future').

It is worth quoting briefly from the literature to indicate the flavour of technical assessments of SDI:

> It will be extremely complex, impossible to test, and will inevitably fail when it is needed – or before. (Nelson and Redell, 1986)

> It is almost impossible to validate models of situations and events that have never occurred.... How do we test for what may have been overlooked, omitted or misjudged? (Hertz, 1986)

> SDI software has two strikes against it from the outset. It can't be fully specified and it can't be adequately tested. (Williams, 1986)

In fact, software issues should lead the list of serious criticisms of the SDI programme. (Williams, 1986)

The upshot is that humans are being taken out of the decision-making loop, yet they live on the receiving end – where the 'kill power' goes. . . . I won't even let my printer go for five minutes without double-checking to make sure it hasn't screwed up. (Newquist, 1987)

. . . many computer scientists believe that systems of the sort being considered by the SDIO cannot be built. (Parnas, 1985)

We have worked on some of the most reliable systems in the world, and based on our experience, we would not trust any SDI implementation. (Bell Labs' Karl Dahlke, quoted by Schatz, 1987)

Technical and political realities have brought the dream down to Earth. (Price, 1988)

The 'political realities' need not detain us, though it is interesting to remember that launch-on-warning had been attacked in the United States as unconstitutional, since only Congress is legally entitled to make the decision to declare war. Moreover the 'defensive' posture of SDI has now largely been abandoned. In January 1989 it was announced that the SDI Miracl (Mid-Infrared Advanced Chemical Laser) system has been assigned a new strategic mission of destroying enemy satellites, a clearly offensive role.

The momentum of SDI suggests that, despite all the objections, some sort of system will be deployed in two or three decades from now. Hopefully, it will not be triggered by mistake, penetrated, or called upon to display its talents.

SUMMARY

This chapter has provided a brief overview of the Strategic Defence Initiative (SDI or 'Star Wars') concept, with attention to background aspects and some of its main functional features (eg the likely reliance on a 'launch-on-warning' facility).

A main aim has been to represent SDI as a paradigm example of a large computer-based facility in which, because of the need for fast response, human beings will increasingly be taken out of the decision-making loops; and where system failure could have grave consequences for human survival.

The perennial topic of computer bugs has been discussed as relevant to system reliability in general and to how much credence can be put on a complex computer-based military system designed to enhance human safety. The question of how Trojan horses or computer viruses may impair the operation of SDI systems is also raised.

Objections – mainly technical rather than political – to SDI are cited, but the objections should not be seen as only applicable to computer-based military facilities. They relate also, *mutatis mutandis*, to other large computer systems that have a social impact and where failure can result in hazard to human beings. Unreliable software (in the age of complex evolving systems) and insecure computer applications (in the age of the virus) are widely relevant to many types of activity in the developed world.

8 The Future

The future of software reliability and system security will, in important respects, resemble the current situation: increasingly complex system will face a spectrum of (traditional and new) threats, with solutions inevitably one step behind. There may be a reluctance among managers to give reliability/security a proper place in defined procedures and investment strategies. Some unlucky firms, hit hard by inadvertent or deliberate damage, will concentrate corporate minds.

It is obvious that reliability and security topics will be influenced by the shape of technological developments. We will continue to see increases in computer power, with relative decreases in the cost of hardware. Most solid-state circuits will be based on silicon but other substances (eg gallium arsenide) will establish an increasingly secure presence. Architectural changes will affect system design, probably with increased parallelism and configurations influenced by progress in such areas as data flow architectures and neurocomputing. And new computing options – using biochips, optic fibres, other optical components, etc – will become available.

New programming languages and techniques will emerge, with frequent refinements – many of them automated – to the familiar systems-development life cycle. Efforts will be made to standardise* aspects of software generation, to improve

*See, for example, the interesting discussion of 'standard 00–55' (intended to cover all software for potentially dangerous military systems) given by Darrel Ince, Professor of Computer Science at the Open University (see *The Independent*, 30/1/89, p 13)

reliability, particularly in areas that may pose a threat to human life. Formal methods will continue to be adopted where appropriate, but it will become increasingly evident that many areas of systems development will remain immune to the advantages of a nicely formal approach. Requirements specifications will continue to be, to a greater or lesser extent, inadequate – unable to reflect *totally* the requisite real-world conditions. Testing will only focus on a proportion of the functional possibilities, and so program correctness will never be established with absolute certainty. Maintenance, moreover, will inevitably introduce further system faults, or changes whose consequences may not be fully known until months or years into the future.

In short, there will always be bugs in complex computer software. This simple fact should be remembered when computers are given increased autonomy in applications where system failure would be hazardous to human life.

Hackers, virus makers et al, like bugs, will always be around (in the happily censorious tones of a televised computer pundit, BBC2, 1 February 1989 – 'there will always be people with twisted minds'), but such freelancers will not represent the only type of threat to system security. There may be good military reasons for sending a virus to foul up the enemy's computer networks; and companies may have an interest in using viruses to wipe out the databases of a competitor. Virus makers may come to be employed by large respected organisations in order to disseminate viruses and to track down incoming ones.

There is also the fact that many existing viruses have by no means 'worked through' their possible effects: it is likely that there are more shocks in store. And to the family of existing replicating viruses must be added the ones that are being launched on their merry way as I write and the ones that will be hatched tomorrow. The virus maker has a peculiar security: he/she can work quietly and anonymously, plotting great consequences for computer networks around the world (or planning smaller effects in local systems) – it is inevitable that bright young computer buffs should see a challenge in this, and that in due course certain companies and other organisations should see an advantage in climbing on the bandwagon.

The future then is one of massively increased technological complexity, with computers increasingly being given decision-making power over human lives. In circumstances where software can never be known to be absolutely correct, and where individuals and organisations have an incentive to penetrate computer systems that can never be known to be absolutely secure, there is no room for complacency.

References

CHAPTER 1

Aaronson A and Carroll J M, The answer is in the question: a protocol study of intelligent help, *Behaviour and Information Technology*, Volume 6, Number 4, 1987, pp 393–402

Astrop A, Factory of the future is no place for man, *Machinery and Production Engineering*, 21 November 1979, pp 23–26

Chester M, Robotic software reaches out for task-oriented languages. The goal: to remove all human supervision, *Electronic Design*, 12 May 1983, pp 119–129

Kull D, Wall Street kills the messenger, *Computer and Communications Decisions*, December 1987, pp 72–74, 104

Lernoux P, *Cry of the People*, Penguin Books, 1982

Liang T-P and Jones C V, Design of a self-evolving decision support system, *Journal of Management Information Systems*, Volume 4, Number 1, Summer 1987, pp 59–82

Mantelman L, Orchestrating people and computers in their networks, *Data Communications*, September 1987

Runzic N P, The automated factory – a dream coming true?, *Control Engineering*, April 1978, pp 58–62

Sweet P, Adapt or die, *Computing*, 6 August 1987

Townsend K, Soft options for the planners, *Computing*, 10 December 1987, pp 43–55

Williamson M, Artificial intelligence takes a stand on the factory floor, *Computerworld*, 6 July 1987, p 83

Witkowski M, Man-machine clanks into step, *Practical Computing March 1980, pp 82–89*

CHAPTER 2
Abbott J, Software Testing Techniques NCC Publications, 1986

Barr A and Feigenbaum E A, *The Handbook of Artificial Intelligence*, Volume 1, Pitman, 1981

Chantler A, *Programming Techniques and Practice*, NCC Publications, 1981

Cho Chin-Kui, *An Introduction to Software Quality Control*, John Wiley, New York, 1980

Gibbons T K, *Integrity and Recovery in Computer Systems*, NCC Publications/Hayden Book Company, 1976

Gilb T, *Design by Objectives*, North-Holland, 1987

Macro A and Buxton J, *The Craft of Software Engineering*, Addison-Wesley, 1987

Martin J, *Security, Accuracy and Privacy in Computer Systems*, Prentice Hall, 1973

McCall J A, An assessment of current software metric research, *Proceedings EASCON80*, IEEE, 1980, pp 323–333

Myers G J, *Software Reliability*, John Wiley, New York, 1976

Perlis A, Sayward F and Shaw M, *Software Metrics: an Analysis and Evaluation*, MIT Press, 1981

Reiffer D J, *Increasing Software Productivity*, Conference, London, 22–23 April 1982, Institute of Data Processing Management

Sommerville I, *Software Engineering*, Addison-Wesley, 1985

Watts R, *Measuring Software Quality*, NCC Publications, 1987

Yourdon E, *The Causes of System Failures*, Modern Data, February 1972

CHAPTER 3

Computer Disaster Casebook, BIS Applied Systems Ltd, 20 Upper Ground, London SE1 9PN, 1987

Campbell D, Keep your secrets, *Personal Computer World*, January 1989, pp 142–146

Charlton J, Sexy sector which can't be faulted, *Computer Talk*, 15–28 February 1988, p 5

Drysdale C, Making cents of security, *Office Equipment*, August 1988, pp 15, 19

Everett H R and Gilbreath G A, A supervised autonomous security robot, *Robotics* 4, 1988, pp 209–232

Harrison E S and Schmitt E J, The structure of System/88, a fault-tolerant computer, *IBM Systems Journal*, Volume 26, Number 3, 1987

Hewitt V, Dp room blaze leaves shipping from all at sea, *Computing*, 1 December 1988, p 6

Saari J and Parker D B, New baseline methodology in reviewing security – experiences from the USA and Finland, *Infomation Age*, Volume 11, Number 1, January 1989, pp 19–24

Security and the 1984 Data Protection Act, Guidance for Computer Users, NCC Publications, 1987

System security: manage the idiots before going for the gropers, *FinTech Electronic Office*, 118, 30 November 1988, pp 1–2

Wood C C, A context for information systems security planning, *Computers and Security*, Volume 7, Number 5, October 1988, pp 455–465

Wood M B, *Introducing Computer Security*, NCC Publications, 1982

Wood M B, *Fire Precautions in Computer Installations*, NCC Publications, 1986

Wood M B, *Guidelines for Physical Computer Security*, NCC Publications, 1986

CHAPTER 4

Baird B J, Baird L L and Renaurs R P, The moral cracker?, *Computers and Security*, Number 6, 1987, pp 471–478

Bologna J, Soviet white-collar crime and criminal justice, *Computers and Security*, Number 7, 1988, pp 553–556

Brill A, The great computer swindle, *Security Gazette*, December 1988, pp 57–58

Computer Disaster Casebook, BIS Applied Systems, 20 Upper Ground, London SE1 9PN, 1987

Dennis T, Why professionals are feeling a bit hacked off, *Computing*, 18 February 1988, pp 24–25

Doswell R and Simons G L, Fraud and Abuse of IT Systems, NCC Publications, 1986

Gliss H, Hackers attack 'secure' international network, *Transnational Data and Communications Report* October 1987, pp 5–6

Hacking into history, *TeleLink*, June 1986, pp 40–52

Shelton E, DEC hackers' trail of havoc hits Leeds, *Computing*, 5 January 1989

Wood M B, *Introducing Computer Security*, NCC Publications, 1982

CHAPTER 5

Alexander M, Virus ravages thousands of systems, *Computerworld*, 7 November 1988, pp 1, 157

Anderson I, Viral invader spreads havoc in American computers, *New Scientist*, 12 November 1988, p 24

Betts M, Virus 'benign' nature will make it difficult to prosecute, *Computerworld*, 14 November 1988, p 16

Burnham B W, *Virus Threat and Secure Code Disribution* US Department of Energy Computer Security Group Conference, Report No SAND–85–0529C; CONF–850428–1, 1985, pp 1–4

Cohen F, Computer viruses, *Computer Security: A Global*

Challenge (Proc. 2nd IFIP Int. Conf. on Computer Security Elsevier Science Publishers B.V., 1985, pp 143–159

Cohen F, Computer viruses, theory and experiments, *Computers and Security*, 6, 1987, pp 22–35

Davis F G F and Gantenbein R E, Recovering from a computer virus attack, *The Journal of Systems and Software*, 7, 1987, pp 253–258

Dembart L, Attack of the computer virus, *Discover*, 5, 11, 1984, pp 90–92

Dewdney A K, Computer recreations: in the game called Core War hostile programs engage in a battle of bits, *Scientific American*, 250, 5, 1984, pp 14–22

Fak V, Are we vulnerable to a virus attack? A report from Sweden, *Computers and Security*, 7, 1988, pp 151–155

Gibson S, Effective and inexpensive methods exist for controlling software viruses, *InfoWorld*, 9 May 1988, p 51

Goodwins R, Understanding the minds behind the viruses, *Computer Fraud and Security Bulletin*, Volume 10, Number 7, 1988, pp 3–4

Highland H J, Data Physician – a virus protection program, *Computers and Security, 6, 1987, pp 73–79*

Highland H J (i), An overview of 18 virus protection packages, Computers and Security, 7, 2, 1988, pp 157–163

Highland H J (ii), The BRAIN virus: fact and fantasy, *Computers and Security*, 7, 4, 1988, pp 367–370

Hilton P, US virus sends chills down UK networks, *Datalink*, 14 November 1988

Joyce E J, Time bomb: inside the Texas virus trial, *Computer Decisions*, December 1988, pp 38–43

Keefe F, Checkpoints against viruses, *Computerworld*, 19 September 1988, p 55

Lammer P, Protection from infection, *Systems International*, June 1988, pp 75–76

Murray W H, The application of epidemiology to computer viruses, *Computers and Security*, 7, 2, 1988, pp 139–150

Nilsen D L F, Live, dead, and terminally ill metaphors in computer technology, or who is more human, the programmer or the computer? *Educational Technology*, February 1984, pp 27–29

Pozzo M M and Gray T E, An approach to containing computer viruses, *Computers and Security*, 6, 1987, pp 321–331

Rosenberg R, Internet virus aftermath: is tighter security coming?, *Data Communications*, December 1988, pp 52–54

Roszak T, The Cult of Information, Lutterworth Press, 1986

Shock F J and Hupp J A, The 'worm' programs – early experience with a destributed computation, *Communications of the ACM*, 25, 3, 1982, pp 172–221

Wood C C, The human immune system as an information systems security reference model, *Computers and Security*, 6, 1987, pp 511–516

CHAPTER 6
Cohen F, Ethical issues in computer virus distribution, *Computers and Security*, 7, 1988, pp 335–336

Davenport W H, *The One Culture*, Pergamon Press, 1970

Durham T, The perils of polluted software, *Computing*, 11 February 1988, pp 26–27

Foreniski T, Vote of no confidence in systems, *Computing*, 17 November 1988, p 20

Goyal A and Lavenberg S S, Modeling and analysis of computer system availability, *IBM Journal of Research and Development*, November 1987, pp 651–664

Ince D, Unravelling the evidence for the prosecution, *Computing*, 3 November 1988, pp 32–33

Joyce E, Software bugs: a matter of life and liberty, *Datamation*, 15 May 1987, pp 88–92

Lamb J, Crashing computers plague flight controllers, *New Scientist*, 10 September 1987, p 40

Lawrence A, On a wing and a prayer, *Computing*, 27 October 1988, pp 26–27

Martin B, Managing faults, *Systems International*, August 1987, pp 45–46

Perry R, *The Programming of the President*, Aurum Press, 1984

Regan D T, *For the Record, From Wall Street to Washington*, Hutchinson, 1988

Saltman R G, Accuracy, integrity and security in computerised vote-tallying, *Communications of the ACM*, October 1988, pp 1184–1218

Shelton E, A terrorist tool of tomorrow?, *Computing* 21 April 1988, p 15

Speller G J and Brandon J A, Ethical dilemmas constraining the use of expert systems, *Behaviour and Information Technology*, 1986, pp 141–143

Staines A, Confused? You will be, *Practical Computing*, September 1987, pp 81–82

Tate P, Risk! The third factor, *Datamation*, 15 April 1988, pp 58–63

Wagenaar W A, The psychological costs of master computer, *Datamation*, 1 July 1985, pp 157, 159

Warner E, Expert sustems and the law, *High Techniology Business*, October 1988, pp 32–35

Warren P, Killing machines, *Computer Talk*, 15 February 1988, p 1

Wray T, The everyday risks of playing safe, *New Scientist*, 8 September 1988, pp 61–65

CHAPTER 7
Baker D, The making of star wars, *New Scientist*, 9 July 1987, pp 36–41

Boehm B W, *Software Engineering Economics*, Prentice-Hall, 1981, p 383

Borning A, Computer system reliability and nuclear war, *Communications of the ACM*, February 1987, pp 112–131

Frenkel K A, Brian K Reid, A graphics tale of a hacker tracker, *Communications of the ACM*, October 1987, pp 820–823

Hertz D B, Will the force of Star Wars be with you?, *Computer News*, 19 June 1986, p 10

Myers W, Can software for the Strategic Defence Initiative ever be error-free?, *Computer*, November 1986, pp 61–67

Nelson G and Rendell D, The Star Wars computer system, *Abacus*, Volume 3, Number 2, 1986, pp 8–20

Newquist H, Star Wars: when imperfect man strives to make perfect machines, *Computerworld*, 30 November 1987, pp 17–18

Parnas D L, Software aspects of strategic defence systems *Communications of the ACM*, December 1985, pp 1326–1335

Pike J, Star wars: the impossible dream, *New Scientist*, 1 September 1988, pp 47–52

Putnam L H, Putnam D T and Thayer L P, Quality in software is free (almost), *Proceedings of the International Society of Parametric Analysts*, Seventh Annual Conference, May 1985, 37 pp

Schatz W, Testing 'Star Wars' packs may be SDIO's biggest fight, *Datamation*, 1 December 1987, pp 45–50

Williams T, Defence systems – the high road of SDI, *Computer Design*, July 1986, pp 123–128

Appendix 1

Update

GENERAL

The importance of reliable and secure computer systems continues to be emphasised in 1989, and it is obvious that the concern will develop further in the 1990s. The British Computer Society (quoted by Mary Fagan, *The Independent*, 14 February 1989) has emphasised that there is an urgent need for better ways of assessing the safety of 'critical' computer systems, particularly those in medical equipment, aircraft, railway signals and nuclear power plants. It is recognised that Safety Related Computer Systems (ie those that can lead directly to human injury if they go wrong) may be so complex that their safety cannot be guaranteed. The BCS has proposed that the Government set up a certifying body for the registration of safety-critical systems.

Martyn Thomas, who chaired the BCS committee on safety-critical systems and who works for the software company Praxis, has acknowledged that there is a level of complexity beyond the scope of current skills in safety assessment ('We need to decide how we are going to draw that line. It is important for society that there is some check'). He draws attention to the fact that the inquiries into the Pressurised Water Reactor at Sizewell B and into the proposed PWR at Hinkley Point have both failed to consider the question of certifying the computer systems involved in reactor safety.

It is also clear that computer crime will become an increasing problem as computer systems become more widespread. The trend is well noted in headlines in both the technical and general press. Thus 'Burglars swap crowbars for computers' (*New Scientist*, 8 April 1989), according to the National Center for Computer Crime Data in Los Angeles. It is estimated that computer crime costs the United States around $555 million each year. Similarly, 'Crooks abandon banks for rich City pickings' (*Computer Weekly*, 27 April 1989). Here it is emphasised that the security of personal computers in the City of London is so poor that the loopholes offer 'easy access to millions'. Police are currently investigating crimes involving up to £100 million.

In such circumstances there is mounting international pressure for legislation to control hacking and related activities. For example, the Dutch Advisory Commission on Investigation (RAC), in its report *Information Technology and Investigations*, recommends increased government investment to tackle the problem of computer crime (reported in *Transnational Data and Communications Report*, March 1989). This is one example of a growing awareness of the problems caused by computer crime in developed societies (see also Hackers below).

IS SOFTWARE RELIABLE?

The question of computer reliability is similarly addressed by Peter Mellor (*New Scientist*, 11 February 1989, pp 52-55). Here a graph based on a software reliability model shows the number of new bugs found per 1000 seconds of running a program. It is estimated that the number of new bugs per thousand seconds at the end of the observation is 6.9 (after 3000 seconds, 2.47 bugs per 1000 cpu seconds). Mellor comments: 'Surprisingly, though, manufacturers rarely take potential software failures into account when assessing the reliability of a complex system.' And the importance of software reliability in safety-critical systems is emphasised (we should 'question the wisdom of continuing to increase our dependence on software when life is at stake'). In the same spirit, Tony Durham (writing in *Computing*, 23 February 1989) quotes Julian Hilton, director of the audiovisual centre at the University of East Anglia, to the effect that it is 'absolutely out of the question' to remove all error from the system. For this reason, 'you must design systems that constantly maintain human vigilance'.

Similarly, an article in *The Independent* (Science and Technology section, 8 May 1989), addresses current efforts to make computer software more reliable. In particular, work at the University of Edinburgh's Laboratory for the Foundations of Computer Science (LFCS) is surveyed. Efforts are being made to develop a mathematical theory of programming and to apply the results to software reliability and other topics.

Again it is worth emphasising the social importance of safe computing. We have already referred to the apparent failure to give adequate attention to computer-system safety in enquiries relating to UK nuclear power stations. In this connection it is also worth considering Watts (1989), 'Software row dogs nuclear power plans'. It is stressed that after a decade of deliberation, Britain's Nuclear Installations Inspectorate (NII) is 'still not satisfied with the software designed to protect Britain's latest generation of nuclear reactors from accidents'.

We have already seen that various types of social disaster and threat are directly related to malfunctions in computer systems (see Chapter 6). It is also the case that automated systems that function satisfactorily can be associated with catastrophe if the man/machine symbiosis is not developed to embody fail-safe characteristics. There have been suggestions that two recent disasters were related to how computer systems, working in conjunction with human beings, were designed to operate.

The first example concerns the worst oil spill in US history, following the crash of the Exxon Valdez. An article by John Lichfield (1989) carries the headline, 'Crew's attempts to save spill tanker over-ridden by computer', and it is suggested that the collision of the massive tanker with Bligh Reef in Prince William Sound was caused by the crew's failure to switch off the computer auto-pilot.

The second example is the appalling tragedy at Hillsborough (Leeds, England) in April 1989, when ninety-five football supporters were crushed to death. There is still debate about the causes of this disaster, but it has been suggested that a computer count was made of the fans passing through the turnstiles, but with no indication of the *distribution* of the people in the ground. In this way, officials and police may have wrongly concluded that there was room for more people in areas that were already full.

Computer system reliability and well-conceived system design are not simply academic niceties. They are essential if human beings are not to be subject to a growing range of life-threatening hazards.

SECURITY

System reliability is usually taken to relate to the effectiveness of systems designed with 'good intent': here systems fail because of human incompetence rather than through human malice and mischief. Deliberate efforts to penetrate or sabotage systems are the concern of those designers interested in maximising the levels of computer security. Hackers and virus makers (see below) threaten system security in many different ways. It is worth emphasising that many simple security measures can be observed – 'never display passwords or pass them on to a colleague' (*Computing*, 2 March 1989).

Cases continue to be reported (in both the technical and general media) of where individuals have penetrated computer systems for various purposes. One example concerned a woman who worked in the Department of Education and Science (cited in *The Independent*, 9 March 1989). She wanted to visit her son in Australia — and so invented an imaginary school on the department's computer, so that she could channel funds to her own bank account. Any adequate security strategy should aim to discourage or detect such incidents.

Today computer systems security is a vast international business. For example, consider the recent Frost and Sullivan report, *Access Control Systems in Europe* (profiled in *Security*

Gazette, April 1989). Here it is suggested that $2 billion a year is being spent in Europe on access control equipment. And security has many other aspects.

High-speed chips are now being developed to facilitate encryption, one approach in the battle against penetration of military and commercial systems (see the report in *Comms Monthly*, April 1989). Encryption options for PCs are also discussed by Jackson (1989), and a listing is included of specific security products.

System protection can also be offered by 'smart cards' (Fifield, 1989), credit cards with implanted microprocessors programmed to provide user authentication and to add electronic signatures to transactions. Already such cards, a barrier against computer crime, have brought commercial benefits in banking, insurance, electronic funds transfer and other sectors.

If disaster, maliciously caused or not, does strike the computer site then various software systems are available to help with recovery. The ARISE facility, for example, is profiled in *Software World* (Volume 20, Number 2). This system is intended to aid planning for, and recovering from, a disaster; and to automate the recovery of applications at the restore site, and at the home centre after the disaster.

Already a few companies collapse every year as a result of computer failure – and there will be more as dependency on computing grows in the years ahead. As well as the many practical security measures that can be taken, companies can also insure (see, for example, the discussion in *The Independent*, 8 May 1989). Whatever route is taken to maximise security there are inevitable trade-offs and nothing is perfect.

HACKERS

In March 1989 a dossier compiled by Emma Nicholson, Conservative MP for West Devon, was presented to the Prime Minister as part of a growing campaign to tighten the law on the abuse of computer information. Cases cited in the dossier include:

- interference with medical records (two deaths have been blamed on interference with a computer in a hospital intensive care unit);

- breaches of nuclear security (in December 1986, hackers penetrated CERN nuclear accelerator computers);

- examples of industrial espionage;

- bogus bookings at travel agents;

- civil aircraft vulnerable to viruses and other forms of interference.

It is stressed that hackers may not be content only with copying information. Thus Victor Smart (in an article, 'New-era Hackers Put Lives at Risk', in the *Observer*, 12 March 1989) points out that once access is gained to a computer system, an intruder may be interested in corrupting or destroying data. And it has also been suggested that hackers may threaten national security by supplying sensitive information to a potential enemy.

It was reported in March 1989 that West German counter-intelligence had uncovered a spy ring centred on computer hackers who may have supplied the Soviet Union with secret military and economic information. The North German Broadcasting Network (NDR) reported that thousands of computer codes, passwords and programs, allowing access to sensitive Western computer centres, had been obtained and passed on by the hackers. The perpetrators were eventually exposed by Dr Clifford Stoll, a Californian astronomer, who set up a computer 'sting' operation (see *The Independent*, 4 March 1989, p 10).

The possibility of military and industrial espionage by means of computer system penetration has encouraged many observers to urge that hacking be made illegal. The UK CBI has said that computer hacking should be made a criminal offence. (One estimate is that computer fraud costs British business around £30 million a year, though the various types of computer disasters are reckoned to cost much more). The CBI, responding to the Law Commission's paper on computer misuse, has made six recommendations:

- hackers should be tried by juries;
- the concept of 'criminal damage' should cover computer programs and data, and take account of computer viruses;
- laws should be framed to prevent hackers operating across country boundaries;
- the offence of obtaining unauthorised access should include such things as computer eavesdropping;
- unsuccessful hacking, like successful attempts, should be a criminal offence;
- confidential commercial information should be protected by civil remedies for loss or damage caused by hackers.

By March 1989, hacking had been outlawed in Canada, Sweden, France and the US. It is not yet an offence in Britain unless accompanied by damage (such as fraud or theft). In January 1989 the Jack Report on banking law suggested that hacking be outlawed, and the UK Law Commission is expected to make firm proposals this year. In the mean time Emma Nicholson's campaign is sure to continue. She is currently pressing for computer hacking to be included in the next Queen's speech (autumn, 1989), though she is critical of evident apathy in this area (quoted in *Computing*, 4 May 1989). At the same time she claims that Scotland Yard's fraud squad is supporting the idea that hacking should become a criminal offence. In Australia, for instance, a government committee has proposed that hackers should face up to ten years in jail.

There is also opposition to the Nicholson campaign. Terence Wright (1989), for example, argues that her proposed anti-hacking Bill is already out-of-date. Similarly, Hugo Cornwall (1989), author of *Datatheft* and other security books, suggests that the proposed legislation is ill conceived ('We'll be lucky to see one computer-specific bit of law reform every five years. Do we really want to see Ms Nicholson's poorly researched bill in that slot?'). Matthew May (1989) argues that a hacking law could in fact weaken security.

However, it does seem clear that the problem of hacking (and computer viruses – see below) will increase in the future. In April 1989, David Bicknell reported that a hacker had caused a breakdown of an IBM 4381 used by the Bristol and West Building Society. And the British Computer Society has identified many types of financial loss caused by hacking (see the report in *Computing*, 20 April 1989). Victor Smart (1989) stated that, according to reliable sources, KGB agents 'are being tutored by British hackers in the latest techniques of breaking into sensitive computer systems'.

It is also worth noting that hackers (and computer viruses) can be blamed when in fact problems are caused by other factors. And claims that systems are prone to penetration are often disputed by system suppliers. *The Sunday Times* claimed that hackers can break in to the Mercury network computer and make calls at the expense of the subscribers. Mercury commented that this suggestion was 'about as misleading as you can get' (quoted in *Comms Monthly*, April 1989).

VIRUSES

Tony Fainberg (in *New Scientist*, 4 March 1989) provides a useful overview of viruses and related phenomena. He suggests that the terms 'virus' and 'worm' derive from science fiction, from David Gerrald's 'When Harlie Was One' (published in 1972) and from John Brunner's 'The Shockwave Rider' (1975) — respectively. Particular attention is given to the Morris 'worm' deposited in Arpanet (see Chapter 5). In a supporting article, Joe Hirst identifies the two main types of viruses:

- parasitic viruses (for example, the Jerusalem virus) that attach themselves to other programs and proliferate via the storage media, usually disks;

- boot viruses, typically positioned in the boot sector of a floppy disk and spreading as disks are moved from machine to machine.

A detailed chronology of events for the spread of the

Arpanet virus is given in *Computers and Security* (February 1989) for 2 and 3 November 1988. It is now recognised that the worm ('virus' and 'worm' are here treated as synonyms) took advantage of a hole in the SMTP *Sendmail* utility.

The same issue (Volume 8, Number 1) of the journal also gives details of the New Zealand Marijuana virus. Here a microcomputer operator suddenly finds that the screen goes blank, after which a new message flashes up:

Your PC is Now Stoned!
!LEGALIZE MARIJUANA!

At the same time, attention was given to an IBM VM alert. Users of IBM mainframes operating under VM and using Release 4 of CMS (Conversion Monitoring System) were urged to beware! The problem was that 'holes' were detected in CMS Release 4, inviting a virus attack.

In February 1989 it was reported (in, for example, *Computer Weekly*, 16 February) that British Rail had admitted suffering serious damage from the 1813 virus. It subsequently handed out free copies of a virus detection program developed in-house. The 1813 virus was detected in a Derby engineering department, the infestation being responsible for the deletion of programs on a local area network affecting about twenty workstations where reliability information on rolling stock is held.

It was also reported (eg in *CW*, 16 February 1989, and in *Computing*, 16 February 1989) that the celebrated virus hunter Dr Alan Soloman had suffered an embarrassing setback: his TestVacc program, designed to examine software for rogue code, was itself attacked by a virus. He was variously quoted as saying 'Clearly, there's somebody out there willing to do malicious things' and 'It is an incredibly evil thing someone has done'. The infested program has now been withdrawn.

Professor Henry Beker, of the London Royal Holloway College, has declared that computer crooks are currently blackmailing large companies for massive ransoms by threatening a virus attack ('I have heard figures of several hundred thousand pounds being demanded' — quoted in *Security Gazette*, March 1989). Companies were unwilling to admit the threats since this would reveal how vulnerable their systems were.

As a means of countering the virus threat, various large UK computer users – British Rail, the Post Office, British Telecom, etc — have together formed the Computer Threat Research Association (COTRA). It is intended that the organisation will work closely with the UK Federation Against Software Theft (FAST) and in due course build links with Europe and the rest of the world. And a further move to protect organisations against computer viruses was the decision by Lloyd's of London to provide an off-the-shelf policy to cover losses caused by computer viruses (reported in the *Financial Times*, 3 March 1989). It is said that the policy, Lloyds of London Systems Perils Policy, is available world-wide except in the US because of the proliferation of viruses in that country (the policy also covers the traditional types of threat to computer systems).

In the March (1989) issue of *Security Gazette* it was revealed how computer crooks were blackmailing large companies for huge ransoms with the threat of infection by computer viruses. The same journal explores viruses further in the April issue, and in May considers possible antidotes. There are now many general descriptive articles in the literature (see for example, Hruska 1989; and the article in *Communications Management*, April 1989).

Some articles focus on particular viruses (for example, the macro virus discussed in detail by Highland, 1989), and some offer advice to computer users who may be worried by the prospect of infestation (eg Bates, 1989; Kelly, 1989; Glen, 1989; and McAfee, 1989).

In April (1989) it was reported that the Computer Threat Research Association (Cotra) was being inundated with requests from micro users worldwide for information on viruses (*Computer Weekly*, 27 April 1989). Cotra chairman Mark Gibbs described the US computer virus problem as 'phenomenal'. In May the world's first major virus-related conference was held in Chicago – for IBM and DEC users. The conference included lectures, briefings, and 'live' demonstrations of hacking and viruses.

CONCLUSION

This brief update highlights the need for on-going research in a rapidly changing sector of a rapidly changing technology. It is increasingly obvious that computers can be wrongly used (*The Sunday Times* (26 March 1989) recently reported on how detailed bomb-making instructions, contained in an electronic version of the *Anarchist Cookbook*, could be read by anyone with a home computer linked to a telephone). And it is equally obvious that computers intended for worthwhile social purposes can fail in operation or be sabotaged in many different ways. We will need to be increasingly aware of the hazards posed by inappropriate, unreliable and insecure computer applications in the years ahead.

SOURCES USED FOR THIS APPENDIX

Abrahams P, A policy to cover computer viruses, *Financial Times*, 3 March 1989

ARISE – The essential software automated disaster recovery system, *Software World*, Volume 2, pp 8–9

Bates J, Putting the virus fears in focus, *Practical Computing*, May 1989, pp 74–76

Bicknell D, Hackers blamed for Bristol shutdown, *Computer Weekly*, 27 April 1989, p 1

Bird J and Birrel I, Elusive 'hackers' on line to be outlawed, *The Sunday Times*, 16 April 1989, p A9

Bird J and Penrose B, Bomb recipes available on home computers, *The Sunday Times*, 26 March 1989, p A3

Burglars swap crowbars for computers, *New Scientist*, 8 April 1989, p 22

Champion M, Professor warned FBI of Pentagon spy hackers in 1986, *The Independent*, 4 March 1989, p 10

Cornwall H, Wrong ways on hacking, *The Guardian*, 13 April 1989, p 31

Durham T, Dramatic developments, *Computing*, 23 February 1989, pp 32–33

Dutch police urged to fight computer crime, *Transnational and Data Communications Report*, March 1989, pp 5–6

Europe's booming \$2 billion access control market, *Security Gazette*, April 1989, p 5

Fagan M, Safety of critical computer systems queried, *The Independent*, 14 February 1989, p 3

Fainberg T, The night the network failed, *New Scientist*, March 4 1989, pp 38–42

Fifield K J, Smartcards outsmart computer crime, *Computers and Security*, 1989, pp 247–255

Glen R, What experts advise for virus defence, *Canadian Datasystems*, March 1989, p 37

Gottfried I S, When disaster strikes, *Journal of Information Systems Management*, Volume 6, Number 2, Spring 1989, pp 86-89

Hacking: counting the losses, *Computing*, 20 April 1989, p 49

Hacking reaches Downing Street, *Computing*, 30 April 1989, p 8

Highland H J, Random bits and bytes, *Computers and Security*, Volume 8, Number 1, February 1989, pp 3–13

Highland H J, A macro virus, *Computers and Security*, 8, 1989, pp 178–182

Hruska I, The complete guide to computer viruses, worms, Trojan horses and . . . the dreaded logic bomb, *Comms Monthly*, April 1989, pp 18–19

Jackson K, Buyers' guide: security, *PC User*, 26 April–9 May 1989, pp 118–123

Kelly M, Treating viruses sensibly, *Practical Computing*, May 1989, pp 72–73

Kelsey T, Criminals come bottom of the computer class, *The Independent*, 9 March 1989

Large P, Outlaw computer hacking – CBI, *The Guardian*, 1 March 1989

Lichfield J, Crew's attempts to save spill tanker over-ridden by computer, *The Independent*, 14 April 1989

May M, How a hacking law could weaken security, *The Times*, 20 April 1989, p 32

McAfee J, The virus cure, *Datamation*, 15 February 1989, pp 29–40

Mellor P, Can you count on computers?, *New Scientist*, 11 February 1989, pp 52–55

Mercury hacking report 'rubbish', *Comms Monthly*, April 1989, p 1

MP slams apathy over hacking, *Computing*, 4 May 1989

New high speed chips help overcome EFTPOS encryption time constraints, *Comms Monthly*, April 1989, pp 22–23

Nicolle L, BR tracks down 1813 virus, *Computer Weekly*, 16 February 1989, p 1

Nicolle L, Crooks abandon banks for rich City pickings, *Computer Weekly*, 27 April 1989

Nicolle L and Maclure C, Anti-hacking lobby urges Bill support, *Computer Weekly*, 27 April 1989

Roberts O, So you think you're insured for more than the hardware, *The Independent*, 8 May 1989, p 16

Secure against the security hype, *Computing*, 2 March 1989

Smart V, Hackers 'teach KGB' to break data secrets, *The Observer* , 14 May 1989, p 6

Smart V, New-era hackers put lives at risk, *Observer*, 12 March 1989, p 5

The dangers of the 'modern army', *Comms Monthly*, April 1989, pp 20–21

The elusive enemy, *Security Gazette*, April 1989, pp 19–20

Virus attack, *Communications Management*, April 1989, pp 26–28

Virus doctor laid low by rogue code, *Computing*, 16 February 1989, p 9

Watts S, Software row dogs nuclear power plans, *New Scientist* , 1 April 1989

Wilson G, Making programming reliable, *The Independent*, 8 May 1989, p 15

Wright T, Hit and miss, *Computer Guardian*, 4 May 1989, p 31

Yard 'backs law against hacking', *The Independent*, 15 May 1989

Index

Note: no references to items in Appendix 1 are included

adversary teams	38
aircraft, safety of	139-142
air traffic control	141-143
anti-virus products	126-127
artificial intelligence	17-18, 19
see also expert systems	
astrology by computer	139
'Big Bang'	20
'bugs' in programs	
see faults in software	
Butler, Samuel	16
certification, software	33
Clarke, Arthur C	22
Clarke, David	133
computer applications	2-5
Computer Disaster Casebook (BIS)	46-51, 69
computer security	
see security, computer	
contingency planning	64-65
correctness of software	33-34
credit checking	131
crime, computer	70-78, 94-95
Cullyer, John	133, 135

data protection legislation 44, 70
decision support systems 14
Denning Mobile Robotics 68
DHSS, UK 132, 137
dial-in connections 87-89, 93-94
disasters 46-51
divers and computers 143
domain testing 39

epidemiology, computer 120-122
Equity Funding case 75
Erewhon 16
expert systems 3-4, 17, 19-20,
133-134, 147

factory production 8, 15-19
fraud 70-78
  see also hacking
faults in computers 27-31
  see also faults in software
faults in software 29, 134-138,
161-162
fault tolerance 66-67, 133-134
financial trading
  see programmed trading
fourth-generation languages 13
future 167-169

globalisation 6
Gold, Steve 83-84

hacking 79-95
  background to 79-81
  discouraging 93-95
  examples of 81-86
  techniques of 87-93
health, computers and 142-143
Home Office, UK 132
human rights 5

industrial action 96-100
input validation 28

insurance   65-66

Komisaruk, Susan   78

legislation   44, 94-95,
  see also data protection legislation   107, 146-147
Lehman, Manny   135-137
life metaphor   108-110, 120-122
logic bomb   103
loops, closing of   11-23
loops, functional   7-9

man/machine symbiosis   9-11
Manufacturing Automation Protocol   18
McDonnell Douglas   15-16, 27
Media Laboratory (MIT)   11
Metropolis   16-17
military systems   21-23, 145-147
  see also Star Wars
Morris, Robert T   119

National Audit Office, UK   131
networks   17
NORAD   81-82

Oakley, Brian   136
Open Sytems Interconnection   18

packet switchstream (PSS)   89-90
partition analysis   39
passwords   91-93
political aspects   137-139
prejudice, computerised   144-145
programmed trading   19-21
program mutation   39
program testing
  see system testing

quality
  assurance   33, 35-39
  control   33
  criteria   31-35
  inspection   33
  measures   31-35

quality inspection   33

radiation treatment   142-143
range of computerisation   2-5
  see also computer applications
Reagan, Ronald   139, 150-152
reliability
  see vulnerability of systems
Rifkins, Stanley   77
risk management   54-57
ROBART robot   68
robots   4, 68

safety
  see vulnerability of systems
'salami' fraud   71
Schifreen, Rob   83-84
scientific management   15
security, automated   67-68
    computer   43-68
    hardware   60-61
    physical   57-60
    software   61-64
    see also crime, computer
        hacking,
        virus, computer
        vulnerability of systems
social impact of automation   129-148
software metrics   34
Software Productivity Consortium   26-27
Solomon, Alan   106, 125
South America   5
SPAN   85
Star Wars   22, 26, 147,
                                                149-165

    background to   149-154
    criticisms of   163-165
    launch-on-warning in   157-159
    problems in   152-153
    profile of   154-157
    reliability of   159-162

security of   162-163
static analysis   39-40
Strategic Defence Initiative (SDI)
    see Star Wars
strikes
    see industrial action
symbolic evaluation   39
system design   28-29
system reliability   25-41
systems evolution   14
system testing   27, 35-40

Taylor, Frederick Winslow   15
terrorist attacks   76-77
testing of systems
    see system testing
test methods, system   36-41
test monitoring   40
theft
    see fraud
Third World   5, 9
threat spectrum   45-46, 95-97
time bomb   103
Trojan horse   103, 108, 110-111

unemployment   12-14
user ids   90-92

validation   32
verification   33, 40
virus, background to   105-108
    computer   103-128
    definition of   111-113
    features of   104, 112-113
    first   114-115
    legislation on   107
    protection from   122-127
virus epidemic?   113-115
viruses by name
    '648'   116
    '1701'   120
    '1813'   116, 120

Amiga   118
Brain   118-119
Christmas tree   117, 118
Friday 13th   120
Internet   119-120
Jerusalem   120
Larry   117
Lehigh   118
NVIR   116
Pakistani   119
retro-virus   116
Scores   119
vote tallying, automated   137-138
vulnerability of systems   132-134
    see also risk management,
          security, computer

War Games   81
weather prediction   143-144
Weizenbaum, Joseph   79-80, 163
Wong, Ken   133
Wood, Michael   58
worm programs   111

Xcon system   17